PRINCES
POETS & PATRONS
THE STUARTS AND SCOTLAND

by Alastair Cherry

EDINBURGH: HER MAJESTY'S STATIONERY OFFICE

Acknowledgements

I should like to thank all those at the National Library of Scotland who have been so helpful and patient during the preparation of this book, particularly Kenneth Gibson, Exhibitions and Publications Officer, who made many valuable and constructive suggestions regarding the text, and whose continuing support contributed to its completion. A special tribute must also be made to Julian Russell of the Department of Manuscripts and to my colleagues in the British Antiquarian Division who assisted me both at the research stage and with the reading of proofs.

The manuscript was prepared by the typing staff of the National Library and many of the photographs by Steve McAvoy, Senior Photographer, to whom warm thanks are also due.

Alastair Cherry
April 1987

Note

There are several ways of spelling the surname Stuart. Until the reign of Mary Queen of Scots the Scottish royal family used the form Stewart, which derived from the name of Walter the sixth Steward of Scotland who served under Robert the Bruce and married the king's daughter, Marjory. She bore him a son Robert, afterwards Robert II, who came to the throne in 1371 as the first of the royal line of Stewart. In the middle of the 16th century this spelling was gradually replaced by the French form Stuart as used by the young Queen Mary influenced by her upbringing in France. This form has remained in general use ever since, particularly in England and Europe, and in the interests of consistency and clarity it has been adopted throughout the text of this book.

Cover illustration:
Portrait of Mary, Queen of Scots by permission of Blairs College, Aberdeen.

Frontispiece:
A fresco of Aeneas Sylvius Piccolomini, later Pope Pius II, visiting James I of Scotland in 1435. It is one of a mural series dating from 1505–8 by Bernardino di Betto (called Pinturicchio. c.1454– 1513) in the Piccolomini Library, Siena Cathedral, depicting events from the life of Pius II.

ISBN 0 11 493388 X

PRINCES
POETS & PATRONS

941.1

CHERRY, A

Hertfordshire
COUNTY COUNCIL
Community Information

13.12.04

6/12

PRINCES, POETS AND PATRONS

Please renew/return this item by the last date shown.

So that your telephone call is charged at local rate, please call the numbers as set out below:

	From Area codes 01923 or 020:	From the rest of Herts:
Renewals:	01923 471373	01438 737373
Enquiries:	01923 471333	01438 737333
Minicom:	01923 471599	01438 737599

L32   www.hertsdirect.org

Contents

Introduction

A royal kind of men – but, at their best, not royal enough.

Thomas Carlyle

History has been described by its critics as the propaganda of the victor, and it would be difficult to deny that there is some truth in this assertion. Historians, like other mortals, are all too easily impressed by success. The victor in battle, as in everyday life, is often praised for his foresight and wisdom, while the elements of chance, the sheer weight of superior military power or greater economic resources and the interplay of human qualities of ruthlessness and mendacity are glossed over or excused in the need to vindicate historical facts. Dubious theories of the inevitability of historical progress are produced to justify the motives and actions of those who, by whatever means, achieve success or simply manage to survive against great odds. The loser, on the other hand, is frequently dismissed as a foolish romantic or at best a poor politician whose ultimate failure seems, with the benefit of hindsight, to have been a foregone conclusion. From this standpoint the tragic history of the Stuarts, who for almost four centuries played a major role in the political, religious and cultural life of Scotland, England and Europe, is proof of their manifest inadequacies and failure as rulers. While this view overlooks much that is valuable in the Stuart heritage it is no more unbalanced than the equally widespread image of the Stuarts that is to be found in romantic fiction and popular history, where there is a strong preference for the violent or melodramatic to the exclusion of much that is worthwhile and enduring. In fact, both of these opposing schools of thought represent extremes, and neither does justice to the cultural achievements and profound influence of a dynasty which numbered amongst its members poets and scholars, patrons of architecture, art and science, musicians, theologians and devout churchmen.

It is the object of this book to draw the reader's attention to the paradoxical character of individual Stuart kings and queens and to emphasize the sharp contrasts between their record as political failures and their influence as cultural achievers, both direct and indirect. So much of Scottish history has been treated negatively or purely romantically in the past that the need to explore its more positive aspects is long overdue.

Of the Stuarts it may be said that they were a gifted race that has bequeathed to the world a remarkable heritage of poetry, drama, music and architecture. The dynasty that produced poets and scholars such as James I and James VI, patrons of the arts and sciences such as James IV and Charles II, and lovers of painting and fine books   such as Charles I and Cardinal York is surely deserving of a better tribute than Thomas Carlyle's dismissive words 'not royal enough'. Carlyle was, of course, a great admirer of successful men of action and could not be expected to have much sympathy for this race of 'artistes manqués'. Yet it is this very lack of success that is the source of the abiding fascination of the Stuarts – a long sorrowful catalogue of personal tragedies, assassinations, executions, violent revolution, lost battles, unsuccessful rebellion and bitter exile; a gloomy saga that once prompted Louis XVI of France to allude to them, with unconscious irony, as 'cette famille infortunée'. Here is a tale composed of tragic miscalculation and recurrent misfortune, a combination that has always exercised a great hold over the human imagination and will no doubt continue to fill the shelves of publishers and booksellers for generations to come.

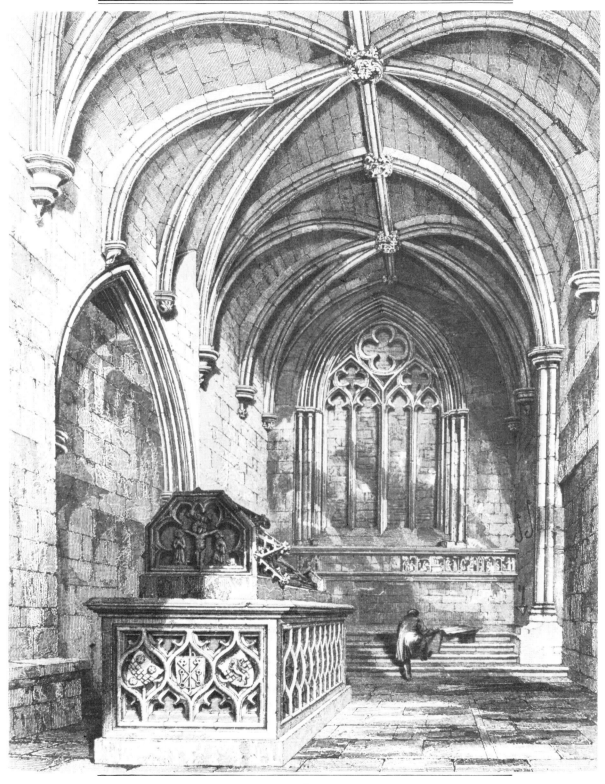

The Early Stuarts: Robert II to James V

*The Stuarts have found few apologists, for the dead
cannot pay for praise; and who will, without reward,
oppose the tide of popularity? Yet there remains still
among us, not wholly extinguished, a zeal for truth, a
desire of establishing right in opposition to fashion.*

Dr Samuel Johnson

To denigrate the Stuarts has long been fashionable, and not only in Dr Johnson's day, for the unsuccessful are rarely popular, except in the pages of romance. The undoubted failure of the Stuart dynasty to adapt to the changes in British society in the 17th and 18th centuries has, however, not only resulted in their denigration: it has also obscured the considerable achievements of earlier Stuart monarchs. Indeed, in this respect it is no exaggeration to say that the sins of the sons and daughters have been visited upon their fathers.

From those who subscribe to the 'success' school of historical thinking and regard the Reformation, the outcome of the Civil War, the Revolution of 1688, and the Union of 1707 as 'good things', the Stuarts command little sympathy. As 'losers' they have mostly attracted a poor press: a long line of historians, from George Buchanan in the 16th century to the present day, has seen to that. In Buchanan's writings, the need to destroy the party that supported Mary Queen of Scots coloured his judgement of her ancestors on the Scottish throne, while in the pages of Whig and Hanoverian historians of a later generation the ever-present Jacobite threat understandably motivated them to belittle the Stuart past, and, by implication, the ancient and distinctive culture of Scotland with which it had been so intimately associated. A similar bias affected even the less prejudiced leaders of the 18th-century Enlightenment, who, despite their genuine attempts to overcome the fierce sectarian hatreds of the past, found it difficult to conceal their distaste for the so-called 'barbarous' Middle Ages. Moreover, although there have always been strong supporters of the Stuarts, many of them have done great damage to their cause by a tendency to envelop their heroes and heroines in a cloud of romantic legend and sentimental trivia, thereby undermining the study of Stuart history as a serious subject.

*Tomb of Marjory
Bruce in Paisley
Abbey.*

It is, however, not only the failures of the later Stuarts that have obscured the achievements of their ancestors, but also the popular assumption that the Middle Ages were hopelessly backward and superstitious, and that the Scots as a people made little contribution to European civilisation until some undefined point after the Reformation. In addition, the fact that comparatively little has survived of Scotland's medieval architectural and artistic heritage has not made it any easier to convince the sceptical of the considerable achievements of that age. How different our perception of medieval Scotland would be if we could still see in their full glory the cathedrals of St Andrews and Elgin, or the abbeys of Holyrood and Melrose, great works of art whose counterparts on a larger scale have survived largely intact south of the border! Similarly, had the Stuart palaces at Stirling, Linlithgow and Falkland – which can stand comparison with some of the lesser châteaux of the Loire – suffered less abuse and neglect, Scotland could now more confidently claim her modest place in the history of Renaissance art. Sadly, the toll of destruction – resulting from the Earl of Hertford's invasion in 1544, the religious iconoclasm of 1559–60, and the civil war that followed Mary's abdication in 1567 – was not confined to buildings, but also extended to their contents, especially libraries. For example, of the royal library which the German bibliophile, Marcus Wagner, lavishly praised on his visit to pre-Reformation Edinburgh little now remains that antedates the reign of James VI.

Nevertheless, it is all too easy to forget that despite the ravages of time some of the major achievements of late medieval Scotland do still stand and have proved to be of lasting value. Foremost among these are the beginnings of modern Scotland's system of education, medicine and law, all of whose foundations were laid in the reigns of the early Stuarts. As far as education is concerned it is remarkable that such a small and comparatively poor country managed, during the disturbances of the 15th century, to found and maintain three universities, all situated at great distance from each other – St Andrews (1411), Glasgow (1451) and Aberdeen (1495). Edinburgh University, although a post-Reformation foundation (1582), can trace its origins back to the regency of Mary of Guise, mother of Mary Queen of Scots, who appointed lecturers in 1556 to instruct scholars in civil and canon law, Greek and the sciences. These lectures were delivered in the Magdalen Chapel situated in Edinburgh's Cowgate, but proved to be short-lived owing to the political and religious unrest that overwhelmed the last years of the Guise regency. Alongside these advances in higher education, an attempt was also made to introduce some degree of compulsory elementary schooling. An act of 1496, in the reign of James IV, sought to persuade all barons and freeholders to put their sons to school at the age of eight, a move that is seen by some educationists as one of the earliest of its kind in Europe. James IV also took an interest in medicine, and was directly responsible for the foundation in 1506 of the Royal College of Surgeons of Edinburgh, while in the reign of his son, James V, the basis was laid for the administration of centralized justice with the foundation of the Court of Session in 1532. All of these institutions owe their origin and initial patronage to the Stuart kings, and still stand as monuments to the enlightenment of Scotland's rulers in the late Middle Ages.

Despite this clear evidence of a body of substantial achievement the romantic excesses of many who favour the Stuarts have often discouraged historians from treating the subject as one worthy of scholarly investigation, thus leading to the neglect of large areas of Scottish history and culture. In her *Scottish Pageant* (1946), Agnes Mure Mackenzie put her finger on the problem. Writing at a time when Scottish history and literature were, in general, considered fit only for teaching in primary schools, she observed: 'No country which ignores its own past can be healthy. . . . We know very little, in fact, of our forefathers; and it is curious, and significant, that the parts of our history of which we know least are apt to be those which do the nation most credit'. Fortunately, since she wrote these words, better informed attitudes have begun to prevail. For instance, in 1982 the National Museum of Scotland's exhibition 'Angels, Nobles and Unicorns', opened the eyes of many Scots to their pre-Reformation heritage, and over the past few decades the establishment of Scottish history as a subject of study in universities and schools has gone a long way towards presenting a more balanced picture of Scotland's medieval past. This change in outlook has not only exposed the myth of cultural backwardness and revealed the true value of Scotland's ancient heritage, in the creation of which the Stuarts played a distinguished part, but has also undermined the old charge of political instability, showing that as a country Scotland in the 15th century was no more unstable than her richer neighbours to the south. England during the Wars of the Roses and France in the Hundred Years War suffered proportionately far more than Scotland did in the struggles between the Stuart monarchs and their unruly subjects. The slaughter in the civil wars between the Houses of York and Lancaster was never matched north of the border, even in the highlands, where clan feuds and raids were an accepted way of life. The tragedies peculiar to the Stuarts and uniquely damaging to their kingdom were of quite another kind, arising from long minorities and sudden death, the latter as likely to be accidental as deliberate. The additional factor of ill-luck, noted by many historians and commented upon by Voltaire in his *The Age of Louis XIV*, is unquestionably a recurrent feature of Stuart history. The long series of royal minorites from James I to James VI is quite exceptional, and helps to explain why the Stuarts were unable to build up the strong centralized government that the Tudors perfected in England. Not until James VI departed for London in 1603 was this tragic pattern finally broken. Whether this record of dynastic tragedies was due more to bad judgement than to bad luck is a matter for debate. Less open to dispute is the powerful attraction which such tragedy has for the poet, the playwright, the artist, the lovers of romance, and the weavers of legend.

Robert II and Robert III (1371–1406)

It cam wi' a lass.

It is in literature and legend that the early Stuart kings and queens of Scotland are most strongly remembered. As befits a tragic tale the opening chapter begins with a tragedy, the death of Princess Marjory, daughter of Robert the Bruce and wife of Walter the High Steward, one of the commanders of the Scottish forces at Bannockburn. She died shortly after giving birth, in 1316, to the future Robert II, the first of the royal line. Her early death had been hastened by a fall from her horse, and it was to her that James V was referring when, two centuries later, he uttered the legendary prophecy on his death-bed at Falkland Palace: 'It cam wi' a lass and it will gang wi' a lass'. Whether or not these were the exact words spoken by the king, they convey something of his desperate state of mind upon hearing the news of the birth of his daughter, the future Mary Queen of Scots, an event which left his kingdom without a male heir. The news hastened James's death as surely as the birth of the future Robert II brought about the end of Marjory Bruce. Her brief appearance in history is commemorated in a richly decorated tomb at Paisley Abbey. Unfortunately, she did not transmit to her son and his immediate heirs the outstanding abilities of her warrior father, and consequently the reigns of the first two Stuart kings (1371–1406) are undistinguished. It is extraordinary that a dynasty which was to produce so many men and women of outstanding gifts began so feebly with two rulers about whom historians have had little to say. Their reigns were years of chaos and disorder. The monarchy could not even control the lawless deeds of its own relations, the most infamous example of this being the burning of Elgin Cathedral in 1390 by Alexander, brother of Robert III, better known by the chilling name 'the Wolf of Badenoch'. This must surely be one of the few occasions in history when a prominent member of the House of Stuart appears in the role of a vandal and not as a patron of the arts! Less substantial as fact but potent as fiction are the mysterious circumstances surrounding the death in 1402 of David, Duke of Rothesay, elder son of Robert III, allegedly at the hands of his uncle, the Duke of Albany. Some say that he was starved to death, and paint a pathetic picture of the young man in the agonies of hunger sucking at the breasts of a compassionate peasant woman through the bars of his prison in Falkland Palace. More picturesque details were added by the 16th-century historian Hector Boece; but most famous of all is the account given by Sir Walter Scott in *The Fair Maid of Perth*. As with Shakespeare's treatment of Richard III, once the hand of a master has been at work it is difficult if not impossible for lesser writers to replace colourful romance with historical fact. Whatever the truth may be about this particular incident it is but one, albeit the first, of a long series of legends that litter the pages of Stuart history to the despair of the historian and the delight of the artist.

Although Robert II and III are rather ineffectual figures, it is in the reign of the former that we first come across evidence of that interest in literature and patronage of writers that was to be so characteristic of the Stuarts. The poet, John Barbour, author of the national epic the *Bruce*, was closely connected with the court of Robert II, and received payments for his literary work including a now lost genealogical poem *The Stewartis Originalle*. As a court official, Barbour occupied a position not unlike that of his contemporary, Geoffrey Chaucer, at the court of Richard II, combining official duties with the cultivation of his art. It is recorded that Barbour presented a copy of the *Bruce* to Robert II, most of it having been composed during the early years of that monarch's reign from 1371–77. Extending the hand of friendship to men of letters was to become an honourable Stuart tradition over the succeeding centuries.

James I: The Poet King (1424–37)

In 1424, with the return from long exile in England of James I, younger son of Robert III, the Stuart line produces one of its

William Bell Scott. Illustrations to the King's Quair. Edinburgh, 1887.

strongest personalities. Uniting in his person the qualities of a man of action with the genius of a poet, he stands in sharp contrast to his incompetent predecessors. James appears on the scene like a lion, and departs from it just as fiercely thirteen years later fighting off assassins' swords with his bare hands. Although some have criticized him for being 'an angry man in a hurry', others are impressed by his strength and sense of purpose. To Thomas Carlyle he is 'a right brave man, the born enemy of all unveracities and dissonances; to whom oppressors, thieves, quacks, and every sort of scoundrels, were an abomination'. A contemporary writer, Jean Chartier, in his *Chronique de Charles VII,* describes him as 'wise, valiant, and a good justiciar'. Like so many of his descendants he had to endure years of exile, but unlike most of them he did succeed in coming into his own again. What is more, he put his period of exile to good use, improving his education while at the courts of Henry IV and V, and composing the romance with which his name is forever associated, *The Kingis Quair.* Most historians praise his talents as a ruler and his accomplishments as a patron of arts and letters. Widely regarded as pious, chaste and upright in his private life, he was firm to the point of ferocity in his pursuit of law and order, a public face of the monarchy to which the Scottish nobility had long grown unaccustomed. Ultimately, this aspect of the king's personality was to cost him his life, and deprive Scotland of one of her most promising rulers, but although his political aims were never fully realized something of his literary genius has survived.

To his literary gifts James added a taste for drawing and painting, as his contemporary Walter Bower informs us. It is said that he played the harp and other musical instruments, 'like another Orpheus', and may even have composed music, an assertion made by Alessandro Tassoni in *De' Pensieri Diversi*. He delighted in the planting of gardens and orchards, in the cultivation of the mechanical arts and in athletics, a combination of talents and interests which he passed on to his great-grandson James IV. His love of learning is well known, and had been inculcated into him as a boy, before he left Scotland, by Henry Wardlaw, the bishop who was largely responsible for founding the University of St Andrews. When James returned from exile he took a keen interest in Wardlaw's foundation, confirmed its privileges and apparently even attended some lectures, although he did consider for a time removing it from St Andrews to a more central position at Perth, a town which he favoured as his capital. Perth, being his favourite town, was chosen as the home for Scotland's only community of the strict order of Carthusians, which he founded shortly after coming to the throne. Influenced by the similar ecclesiastical policy of Henry V in England, this royal foundation of the Perth Charterhouse was a major contribution to the monastic life of Scotland.

The Kingis Quair

It is as a poet that James is chiefly honoured. Controversy about the authorship of *The Kingis Quair* (The King's Book) is now largely a thing of the past, but no other poem can be firmly attributed to him. He may, however, have been responsible for two poems of rustic love, *Christis Kirk on the Green* and *Peblis to the Play*, although in the case of the former some have advanced the claims of James V. His only certain surviving work, the *Quair*, was probably composed towards the end of his imprisonment in England, and about the time of his return to Scotland in 1424. Written in a mixture of Scots and Chaucerian English, this long poem describes his thoughts and experiences as a prisoner, and his love for a noble English woman, Lady Joan Beaufort, cousin of Henry V, to whom he was later married. As a work of literature it has been described as the earliest Scottish poem intended for the court, but of more interest to a modern reader is the intensely personal flavour of the verse, the strength and warmth of the poet's feelings, and the unconventional celebration of married love, all of which set it far apart from the customary stilted conventions of medieval courtly literature. The moment when his love was first awakened by the sight of his future queen walking in a garden below his prison is celebrated in these lines:

> And therewith kest I doun myn eye ageyne,
> Quhare as I saw, walking under the toure,
> Full secretly new cummyn hir to pleyne,
> The fairest or the freschest yonge floure
> That ever I sawe, me thoght, before that houre,
> For quhich sodayn abate, anon astert
> The blude of all my body to my hert.

The freshness and charm of the verse, and the fact that this was one of those rare moments in Stuart history when personal affection and dynastic interest happily coincided, have ensured for the *Quair* a unique position in Scottish literature. Not many of the Stuarts were to share the good fortune of the first James in their marital experiences: too many royal unions had disastrous political consequences, and most are commemorated in verses that rarely rise above the mediocre.

It seems fairly certain that the *Quair* influenced the later Scots poets of the 15th and 16th centuries, but the earliest text known to survive was not found until 1783 when the historian William Tytler discovered it in the Bodleian Library in Oxford, and published it that same year in Edinburgh as *Poetical Remains of James the First, King of Scotland*. A multitude of editions and translations followed in the 19th and 20th centuries, and still continue to appear. The romantic circumstances surrounding its composition have also influenced the visual arts, notably the Victorian artist William Bell Scott who was commissioned by the Boyd family of Penkill Castle in Ayrshire to paint murals of scenes from the *Quair* on the staircase of their castle. These were executed between 1865 and 1868 and later published as etchings in *Illustrations to the King's Quair of King James I. of Scotland* (Edinburgh 1887).

Another artistic memorial of the reign of James I is to be found in a most unlikely location, the cathedral library of Siena in Italy, where the 15th-century artist Pinturicchio painted a superb, if wholly fanciful, fresco commemorating the visit of the Italian diplomat and poet, Aeneas Sylvius Piccolomini, to the Scottish court in 1435. This historic mission does not seem to have been a diplomatic success, but fortunately Piccolomini, who later became Pope Pius II, recorded his experiences in his *Commentaries*, an extremely valuable impression of medieval Scotland. Not much is known of what passed between the Renaissance poet and the Scottish king, but it would be pleasant to think that they found time to turn the discussion away from politics to that of poetry in which they shared a common interest. The portrait of James in the Siena fresco is quite unhistorical, being that of a much older man with a long white beard presiding like a grave doctor of the Church over an elegant

Renaissance court which is set against the idyllic background of a southern landscape (see frontispiece).

The reign of James I came to an abrupt end two years after Piccolomini's visit with the king's brutal murder on February 20th 1437 in the Dominican friary at Perth, a tragedy which gave rise to the tale of Lady Katherine Douglas thrusting her arm through the bars of a door in the royal apartments in a vain attempt to allow the king time to make his escape. So perished one of Scotland's ablest monarchs at the hands of a group of disaffected nobles. Queen Joan, who was severely wounded while trying to defend her beloved husband, took a terrible revenge on his murderers who were quickly brought to justice and put to death after undergoing indescribable tortures exceptional even for that age. The murder inspired a spate of legends, some of which first appeared in the *Dethe of the Kynge of Scotis* written in England a few years later, and also in the *Liber Pluscardensis*. Centuries later Tobias Smollett wrote a tragedy for the stage on this theme entitled *The Regicide: or, James the First, of Scotland* (1749).

Daughters of the Poet King

see plates page 1

The talents of James I did not entirely die with him, but were passed on to his daughters, three of whom are known to have been literary ladies, all married to foreign princes. The eldest, Margaret, married the Dauphin of France, afterwards Louis XI, but died before he became king. Betrothed in 1436 at the tender age of eleven to a man whose unpleasant character has been well drawn by Scott in *Quentin Durward*, Margaret had more than her fair share of Stuart misfortune. Her passion for poetry and her patronage of men of letters, particularly the poet Alain Chartier, brought upon her head a campaign of gossip and slander which seems to have been instrumental in causing her early death in 1445 at the age of twenty; more than a century later Mary Stuart had to endure similar innuendos about her relationship with her Italian secretary, David Rizzio. Poor Margaret was neglected by her cold and indifferent husband and used to sit up all night writing French rondeaux and ballads. In a moment of indiscretion she is supposed to have kissed the lips of the poet Chartier (while he slept) as a demonstration of her admiration for his genius. Predictably, this innocent explanation was not universally believed, but whatever the truth she soon after went into a rapid decline and died. An epitaph on her is included in the *Liber Pluscardensis*, translated into Scots by command of her brother James II. Margaret's own verses have not survived. Her more fortunate sister Isabella, married to Francis, Duke of Brittany, in 1442, was a notable bibliophile, and possessed a number of richly illuminated books of hours, one of which is now in the Fitzwilliam Museum in Cambridge and another in the Bibliothèque Nationale,

see plates page 1

Paris, in which she is portrayed in the company of St Francis. A third sister, Eleanora, married to Sigismund, Archduke of Austria, in 1449, also possessed fine books including an early Italian incunable, an edition of St Jerome's *Epistolae* printed in Rome about 1467. This book was gifted by the archduchess to the monastery at Neustift in the Tyrol, possibly the earliest recorded Scottish provenance in a printed book. A splendid Virgil manuscript in Edinburgh University Library written in Paris by an Italian scribe in the middle of the 15th century is also associated with her; the initials 'P' and 'L' beside the Scottish royal arms in this volume are thought to stand for 'Principissa Leonora'. Art and literature flourished at her husband's court in Austria where there were strong links with leading humanist figures such as Aeneas Sylvius Piccolomini, whom Eleanora may have seen when he visited her father's court in Scotland in 1435. She had literary aspirations and translated into German the French romance *Ponthus and Sidonia*, an edition of which was published in Augsburg in 1483, shortly after her death. A contemporary German writer, Heinrich Stainhowel, dedicated to her his translation of Boccaccio's *De claris mulieribus* (Ulm c.1473).

James II: of the Fiery Face (1437–60)

James II does not seem to have shared the literary tastes of his father or his sisters, being primarily a man of action, tough, energetic and successful, until an unfortunate accident cut short his days and plunged his kingdom into yet another royal minority during which various noble families struggled for ascendancy. Known as 'James of the Fiery Face' because of a large birthmark, he does not seem to have been the kind of personality that attracts the literary imagination, and consequently his reign is not littered with the fictitious accretions that so often attach themselves to the Stuarts. Not that the period is lacking in excitement and tragedy: his reign saw the judicial murder of the young Douglas brothers, victims of the 'Black Dinner' at Edinburgh Castle in 1440, the murder at Stirling twelve years later of another Douglas by the king's own hand, and the final violent scene at the siege of Roxburgh Castle in 1460 when one of the royal cannon accidentally exploded and killed the king who was standing nearby. This incident, familiar to every Scottish schoolboy, impressed itself centuries later upon the childish imagination of Marjory Fleming, Scott's much-loved 'Pet' Marjory. She records it in these lines:

> He was killed by a cannon splinter,
> Quite in the middle of the winter;
> Perhaps it was not at that time,
> But I can get no other rhyme!

More seriously, the keen interest that James II showed in the new invention of artillery was probably responsible for the introduction into Scotland of that legendary piece of ordnance called Mons Meg which can still be seen in Edinburgh Castle and around which numerous improbable tales have been woven.

The marriage in 1449 of James II to the Burgundian Mary of Gueldres not only brought much-needed wealth to the Scottish crown, but also introduced to the court a woman of piety and culture whose artistic tastes were passed on to her son, James III. Her principal claim to fame was the foundation in 1460 of Trinity College Church in Edinburgh, of which only a forlorn fragment has survived, tucked away from sight down a dark close off the High Street. Founded in memory of her late husband, this beautiful church was a fine example of 15th-century Scots architecture and stood originally on the site of what is now Waverley Station. Its demolition in 1848 in the name of progress caused a great outcry at the time and provoked the archaeologist Sir Daniel Wilson in 1853 to compose a verse satire, *The Queen's Choir* (in imitation of *The Kingis Quair*), directed against the North British Railway Company who, in league with the city fathers, were the principal perpetrators of this piece of vandalism. Wilson's literary arrows must have had some effect in shaming those responsible into making reparation, for in 1872 some of the stones of the church, having lain exposed to the elements on Calton Hill for nearly 30 years, were incorporated into the existing melancholy rump as an appendage to a new church dedicated to the Holy Trinity.

The original church is now better known for its association with the famous Trinity panels, part of an altarpiece painted by the Flemish artist Hugo van der Goes, which portrays James III, the son of Mary of Gueldres, his Queen, Margaret of Denmark, and the future James IV. These precious survivals of late medieval art, which somehow escaped the iconoclastic zeal of the Scottish reformers, have been more fortunate in their history than the church that they adorned and can now be seen in the National Gallery of Scotland in Edinburgh, an outstanding example of late medieval Stuart patronage.

James III: A Royal Enigma (1460–88)

The ill-fated and unpopular James III is one of those monarchs about whose character and deeds writers are still divided. With the conspicuous exception of Mary Queen of Scots he has attracted more than the customary trappings of mystery and imagination that surround the early Stuarts.

There can be no doubt that he was a man of cultured tastes like his grandfather, the poet king. Almost certainly he was responsible for commissioning Hugo van der Goes to paint portraits of himself, his queen and his son, and his coinage is the earliest outside Italy to bear a Renaissance portrait of the sovereign. Although records are scanty, his interest in architecture is well recorded and was evident in his patronage of Robert Cochrane, an architect who may have been responsible for commencing the building of the great hall in Stirling Castle, but who certainly met a violent death along with other royal favourites at Lauder Bridge in 1482. In addition to fostering painting and architecture, James was a patron of music, one of his favourites being William Rogers, an Englishman, under whose influence the king may have founded the musical tradition at the Chapel Royal in Stirling. We also know that he presented an organ to Trinity College Church in Edinburgh, and that he was devout in his religious observances and responsibilites, taking a particular interest in the collegiate churches at Restalrig and Tain. This combination of piety, patronage of the visual arts and political misfortune suggests some parallels with Henry VI of England, or more accurately with Charles I, both of whom were equally unsuccessful in dealing with the practical details of government.

James III was fortunate in that both his mother and his wife seem to have been women of strong character, pious and cultured. Margaret of Denmark, whose marriage to him in 1469 brought Orkney and Shetland to the Scottish crown, was the first Scottish queen since St Margaret to be considered for canonization. Shortly after her death in 1486 a petition was sent to Rome urging her cause but, as with the far more controversial case of Mary Stuart a century later, nothing came of this call to raise her to sainthood. However, her good name seems to have spread very quickly, for a biography was soon afterwards published by an Italian, Jacopo Filippo Foresti of Bergamo, in *De plurimis claris selectisque mulieribus* (Ferrara 1497).

There is evidence that James III collected books. In 1467 he paid the royal chaplain for copying the *Travels of Sir John Mandeville,* and in 1471 Anselm Adornes of Bruges presented him with a manuscript account of his journey to Jerusalem. During his reign there are records of payments for prayer-books and a missal for both the king and queen, but none of these seems to have survived. Fortunately there are still in existence several of the books of his tutor, Archibald Whitelaw, who held the office of royal secretary for much of the reign. Whitelaw was a leading humanist and had in his library editions of Lucan, Horace and Sallust. His influence upon the king was no doubt considerable. The reign also saw a flowering of literature which reached its peak under his son, James IV. Many of the poets of this reign who are mentioned in contemporary Treasurer's Accounts as having received pensions, or who are listed by William Dunbar in a later poem (famous for its solemn refrain 'Timor mortis conturbat me'), are now no more than names, their works no longer extant. However, the writings of Robert Henryson, widely regarded as the finest Scottish poet of his day, have happily survived.

Lauder Bridge

To move from a study of the culture of James III to that of his private character and public life is to step upon very uncertain ground indeed. His life and death have attracted an inordinate amount of legend and unsubstantiated gossip. The tales told about him by Pitscottie, Sir David Lindsay, George Buchanan, Drummond of Hawthornden and Scott have passed into the history books and were for long not seriously challenged. Modern historical scholarship has tried to scrape away the myths in much the same way as some English historians have sought to rehabilitate the reputation of Richard III, but the popular impression stubbornly persists of a cultured monarch surrounded by low-born male favourites, despised by his nobles and out of touch with his subjects. Whether he really shared the homosexual tastes that helped to bring Edward II of England to his doom is not certain, but the hanging of his royal favourites in 1482 at Lauder Bridge by his nobles is a historical fact. Picturesque details have been added down the years about this incident, especially the haughty demeanour of Robert Cochrane, the king's 'Prime Minister' and architect, gorgeously dressed and behaving with all the insolence of Piers Gaveston of old toward an infuriated and uncultured aristocracy whose patience had finally broken down. In much the same vein is the famous tale of Archibald, Earl of Angus, declaring defiantly that he would 'bell the cat' when the disgruntled nobles, looking for a spokesman to present their grievances to the king, compared their predicament to that of mice facing a cat! The exact details of what actually happened at Lauder Bridge are far from certain, but the myths had a potent influence on the conduct of the Scottish aristocracy in the following century, and became a useful weapon with which to intimidate the monarchy. A story is told by Sir George Mackenzie of the young James VI being thrashed by his tutor George Buchanan because of his reluctance to write an essay justifying the Lauder Bridge hangings!

Sauchieburn

The death of James III in 1488 at the battle of Sauchieburn while endeavouring to suppress a rebellion of his nobles is another grey area where fact and fiction are hopelessly mingled. The traditional story tells of the king fleeing from the field armed with Bruce's sword, being thrown off his horse, and taking refuge in a peasant's cottage. Calling out for a priest, the injured monarch was supposedly stabbed to death by a passer-by whose identity has never been established. Once again the only certain fact is that the King of Scots was killed in the confusion of a battle in which he vainly tried to assert royal supremacy over his nobility. His fate no doubt gave his successors on the Scottish throne many an uneasy moment and may well have been in the mind of Mary Stuart when she made her fatal, panic-stricken ride to the Solway in 1568 after her defeat at Langside in circumstances not dissimilar to those of Sauchieburn eighty years before. The possibility that the death of her ancestor was an accident and not premeditated may have seemed less likely then than it does now to historians carefully sifting the evidence at a distance of five centuries.

James IV: Monarch of the Golden Age (1488–1513)

The uncertainties that surround the life and personality of James III are noticeably absent from the career of his son and successor, the fourth James, the most able ruler to occupy the Scottish throne since the days of Bruce, and certainly the most popular of the Stuarts. Despite an inauspicious beginning on the field of Sauchieburn, and a disastrous end at Flodden twenty-five years later, his reign is justly regarded as one of the greatest periods in Scottish history, and, in terms of cultural achievement and national prestige, something of a golden age. Combining a love of action with a passion for the arts and sciences, he was the only member of his House between Robert III and Charles I to come to power as a reasonably mature adult. Throughout his comparatively long reign he maintained a degree of peace and stability in his divided country that had not been known for generations, thereby providing the necessary conditions for a flowering of the civilized arts. A charismatic figure, handsome, intelligent, courageous and with an enquiring turn of mind, he greatly impressed a contemporary Spanish visitor to Scotland, Pedro de Ayala, who praised his wide knowledge of languages which apparently included Latin, French, German, Flemish, Italian and Spanish. Ayala also records that James knew the Gaelic, the last Scottish monarch to speak the ancient language of the highlands and islands. To his love for languages he added a zeal for education and learning which made major advances under his rule with the Education Act of 1496 and the foundation, in 1495, of King's College, Aberdeen, the first university in Britain to provide for a chair of medicine. His interest in medicine extended to dentistry where he indulged in a little private practice from time to time! He also persuaded the Town Council of Edinburgh to grant in 1505 a 'Seal of Cause' to the barbers and surgeons, which he confirmed by royal charter the following year in the foundation of the Royal College of Surgeons.

Printing and Alchemy

Anxious to bring to his kingdom the latest advances in the sciences and in the new learning, James was largely responsible for introducing to Scotland one of the major technological innovations of the late Middle Ages: the printing press. A royal charter of 1507 established the first national printing press in the Cowgate in Edinburgh under the management of a wealthy local merchant, Walter Chepman, in partnership with a bookseller and printer, Andrew Myllar, who had received his training in Rouen. On his return to Scotland Myllar brought back French craftsmen carrying with them a gothic typeface that gives to early Scottish printing the distinctive flavour of the 'Auld Alliance'. Little remains of the output of those first Scottish printers, and one can only speculate on what might have been destroyed during the turmoil of the middle years of the 16th century. Fortunately, the earliest product of the Chepman and Myllar press to survive is a unique volume of poetry published in 1508 containing verse by the major Scots poets of the age, William Dunbar and Robert Henryson, an invaluable testimony to the importance of poetry at the court of James IV.

The king's varied interests also included alchemy, showing a scientific bent that is not popularly associated with the Stuarts, who are usually thought of as poets and dreamers. Associated with James in his alchemical studies and experiments was a clever foreigner, John Damian, who, helped by generous royal support,

established a laboratory in Stirling Castle. Damian rose so high in royal esteem that he was given the coveted position of abbot of Tongland in Galloway in order to provide him with the income necessary to carry on with his projects. This appointment brought upon him the enmity of the poet William Dunbar, who had cast longing eyes on the post for himself. Damian's interests extended to aeronautics, a subject which was attracting the attention of Leonardo da Vinci about the same time, but an attempt to fly from the battlements of Stirling Castle failed ignominiously, much to the delight of his detractors, chief among whom was Dunbar, who celebrated the incident with spiteful gusto in a satirical poem, *The fenyeit Frier of Tungland, how he fell in the myre fleand to Turkiland:*

> He schewre his feddreme that was schene
> And slippit owt of it full clene
> And in a myre, up to the ene
> Amang the glar did glyd.

Damian, like many an innovator before and since, was obviously an easy target for glib jokes, but the king's patronage and loyalty towards him cast credit upon James as an enlightened and generous patron.

The Great Michael

Being essentially a man of business, James did not neglect important matters such as trade and defence. He took a keen interest in building up a navy and making visits to the remote western isles of his kingdom, a policy that was followed by his son James V. The pride of James IV's fleet was the 'Great Michael' which, if we are to believe Pitscottie, was the greatest vessel of its day in Scotland, England and France – 'of so great stature, and took so much timber, that, except Falkland, she wasted all the woods in Fife'. Sadly the glory of this great ship was short-lived. After the disaster at Flodden she was sold to France for forty thousand francs.

The 'Aureate Age'

A more complete picture exists of the way of life at the court of James IV than for any earlier Scottish monarch. His court was a place of ceremonial and pageantry, a haven for artists, craftsmen and men of letters. The rich variety of court life is described by Dunbar:

> Schir, ye have mony servitouris
> And officiaris of dyvers curis,
> Kirkmen, courtmen and craftismen fyne,
> Doctouris in jure and medicyne
> Divinouris, rethoris and philosophouris,
> Astrologis, artists and oratouris,
> Men of armes and vailyeant knychtis,
> And mony uther gudlie wichtis:
> Musicianis, menstralis and mirrie singeris,
> Chevalouris, cawanderis and flingaris:
> Cunyouris, carvouris and carpentaris,
> Beildaris of barkis and ballingaris:
> Masounis lyand upoun the land
> And schipwrichtis hewand upone the strand:
> Glasing wrichtis, goldsmithis and lapidaris,
> Pryntouris, payntouris and potingaris.

If the memory of Flodden could for a moment be blotted out, then his reign would truly qualify for the description 'Scotland's Aureate Age'. A golden age it undoubtedly was for poetry, pageantry and music; its most splendid moment being the marriage at Holyrood in 1503 of James to Margaret Tudor, daughter of Henry VII, a union momentous in its long-term consequences which were to bring together the crowns of England and Scotland a century later. No public celebration in medieval Scottish history is so well chronicled. James seems to have been a master of good public relations. Nothing was spared; the festivities lasted for five days and included pageants, banquets, bonfires, jousting, acrobatics and dancing. Dunbar celebrated the marriage in *The Thistle and the Rose*, and welcomed the arrival of the Tudor princess in Scotland with these lines:

> Now fair, fairest, of every fair,
> Princess most pleasant and preclare,
> The lustiest one alive that been,
> Welcome of Scotland to be Queen!

On less formal occasions Dunbar's poetry lifts the curtain on the earthier side of court life and his verses often have a bite and grim humour that puts him on a level with Burns and MacDiarmid. In his

Dance in the Queen's Chalmer the poet mocks the ungainly footwork of courtiers trying to work off the embarrassing effects of over-eating – the humour here is very broad indeed! Elsewhere he complains repeatedly of royal neglect, but despite this seems to have been a favourite of both the king and queen and to have received a regular pension, a generosity that was shared by other men of letters. According to the Treasurer's Accounts, payments were also made to Blind Harry, author of the patriotic epic the *Wallace*, and to John Reid of Stobo who has been credited with the authorship of the anonymous poem *The Three Priests of Peebles*, composed during the reign of James III. Gavin Douglas, the future Bishop of Dunkeld and translator of the *Aeneid* into Scots, dedicated his poem, *The Palace of Honour* to the king, and his allegory, *King Hart*, a version of the Everyman theme, is considered to be a fairly accurate portrayal of the Scottish court. James probably tried his hand at poetry also, and may be the author of verses written in honour of Margaret Drummond of Stobhall:

> Quhen Tayis bank was blumit bricht
> With blossomis bricht and braid,
> Be that river ran I doun richt
> Undir the ryss, I reid.
> The merle melit with hir micht,
> And mirth in morning maid;
> Throw solace, sound, and semelie sicht
> Also ane sang I said.

The lady in question was the favourite mistress of James's youth and he probably intended to marry her, but her early death together with that of her two sisters – possibly by poison – left the way clear for the marriage to Margaret Tudor. James, however, never forgot Margaret Drummond, and had masses said for her soul until the end of his days.

Fine Books

To his interest in the new invention of printing James added an appreciation of beautiful and scholarly books, both printed and manuscript. At the beginning of his reign his father's chaplain, John Ireland, presented him with the *Mirror of Wisdom* written expressly for his instruction, a gentle hint that the new sovereign would be both pious and conscientious! Despite his taste for mistresses James made an effort to be both of these things, and what we know of the royal library certainly suggests scholarly interests and a conventional piety. During his reign there are records of payments for learned texts in printed editions, for printed service books, and for manuscripts, some supplied by scribes within Scotland and others paid for by the king and presented to religious houses in Stirling, Cambuskenneth and Culross. A painter and illuminator in the royal service, Thomas Galbraith, was paid in 1502 for illuminating the

ratification of the marriage contract between James and Margaret
Tudor. Galbraith also received payment for an illuminated Gospel
book and a breviary, possibly intended for use in the Chapel Royal
at Stirling, which had been elevated to the status of a collegiate
church in 1501. An inventory of the service books in the Chapel
Royal compiled in 1505 is still extant and includes among the 28
volumes listed a missal, four antiphonals, and a new gradual gifted
by the abbot of Inchcolm. Undoubtedly the most outstanding
manuscript to survive from this reign is the magnificently illuminated Flemish Book of Hours commissioned by James about the time
see plates page 4 of his marriage. Now in the Austrian National Library in Vienna it is
richly decorated with a high degree of naturalism and attention to
detail. Two miniatures of James and Margaret Tudor show the royal
couple at prayer in attitudes similar to those of his parents James III
and Margaret of Denmark as painted by Hugo van der Goes on the
Trinity College Church panels, possibly indicating a direct influence
on the Flemish artists who were responsible for this splendid Book
of Hours. Also surviving from this period is the Carver Choirbook,
one of the major sources of 16th-century Scottish music. Closely
related to the reorganization of the Chapel Royal at Stirling, it
contains Flemish and English music, as well as the work of the
Scottish composer, Robert Carver, who, besides being a royal
musician, was also a canon of the Abbey of Scone; eight of the
compositions are by Carver himself, including masses and motets.
Another precious relic of royal provenance is the prayerbook of
Alexander, James's eldest illegitimate son, who was appointed
Archbishop of St Andrews in 1504 while still a minor. This gifted
young man, of whom the king was immensely proud, was sent
abroad for part of his education, and had Erasmus as his tutor in
Siena. His youthful promise was cut short at Flodden where he
perished beside his father, a tragic loss lamented by Erasmus in his
Adagia: 'What hadst thou to do with fierce Mars . . . thou that were
destined for the Muses and Christ'.

The Flowers of the Forest

The temptation to paint too rosy a picture of the reign of James IV
must be resisted. Of corruption and intrigue there was no doubt
plenty, but the inescapable impression remains of a society in a
healthy state of economic and cultural expansion united to an
uncommon degree behind a popular and enlightened monarch.
Flodden of course shatters the golden image, that fatal September
day in 1513 when the lamps finally went out for James and his
brilliant court, to be relit again only fitfully in the reign of his even
more unfortunate successor, James V. The extent of the casualties at
Flodden underlines the astonishing amount of support that James
IV, alone among the Stuarts, received from his people. The death
toll – ten thousand according to the English – may have been
exaggerated, but the calamitous effect on the nation's morale was
incalculable, and its influence on song, poetry and legend lives on.

Not until Culloden two and a half centuries later was a military defeat to leave such a deep literary impression upon the Scottish people. The most poignant tribute to this disaster is, by general consent, Jane Elliot's beautiful elegy, *The Flowers of the Forest:*

> I've heard them lilting at the ewe milking,
> Lassies a-lilting before dawn of day;
> But now they are moaning on ilka green loaning;
> The flowers of the forest are a'wede away.

In the sixth canto of *Marmion* Scott too felt the need to add his lament for the passing of the golden days of King James:

> Tradition, legend, tune, and song,
> Shall many an age that wail prolong:
> Still from the sire the son shall hear
> Of the stern strife, and carnage drear,
> Of Flodden's fatal field,
> Where shivered was fair Scotland's spear,
> And broken was her shield!

James V: The Poor Man's King (1513–42)

Since the curtain came down at Flodden there has been a tendency for later writers to falsify the years that went before, much as some

Entry of the Dauphine, Margaret of Scotland, into Tours. (Chroniques de Charles VII.)

Isabella of Scotland and St Francis. (Heures d'Isabeau d'Ecosse.)

Hugo van der Goes.
James III and
Margaret of
Denmark.

post-1914 poets and novelists have romanticized the period before the Great War. As a result, the reign of James V, who came to the throne as a mere infant, is generally compared unfavourably with that of his father. Disadvantaged by the unsettling effects of a long minority and an unsatisfactory education, surrounded by warring factions and largely neglected by a mother whose marital history was almost as complicated as that of her brother Henry VIII, the young king grew up to be a moody, complex, unpredictable and indeed almost schizophrenic personality. Sometimes described as 'James the Ill-Beloved' he seems in fact to have been loved by the common people, but distrusted by his nobles, whose services he neglected. This distrust and neglect were ultimately to be his undoing, but during his short personal reign, from 1528 to 1542, his accomplishments in the civilized arts were considerable, and were enhanced by a rich growth of legend that is intimately associated with him and by which he is chiefly remembered.

The Gudeman of Ballengeich

Like his daughter, the ill-starred Mary, James enjoyed wandering in disguise among his subjects, but his frolics were more than just innocent fun. Amorous adventure rather than egalitarian zeal was probably the main motive for these royal wanderings from palace to cottage. Yet the tradition of James as a 'poor man's king' lives in contemporary literature, which is full of tales of his meetings with millers, tinkers and robbers, some mere inventions, others valuable for the light that they shed on his strange character. Displaying a perverse sense of humour, he would choose a variety of nicknames such as 'The Gudeman of Ballengeich' or 'The King of the Commons', riding by night, often alone, mixing with gypsies and vagabonds and on one occasion narrowly escaping serious injury at the hands of robbers at Cramond Mill near Edinburgh. In this particular episode his rescuer, Jock Howieson, was handsomely rewarded for his services and, the story goes, was afterwards utterly astonished to discover the true identity of the 'Gudeman' when the king chose to reveal himself at a meeting in Holyrood. Some of these escapades had a serious purpose, the enforcement of law and order, a means whereby James could easily familiarize himself with the daily problems of his subjects and thus appear in the guise of a protector; but equally they provided him with easy access to sexual adventures. His immorality was notorious even for that age. Memories of these exploits survive in two poems, *The Jolly Beggar* and *The Gaberlunzie Man*, which were for long popularly attributed to him. Both tell the tale of a man, disguised as a beggar, making a conquest of a country girl. In *The Jolly Beggar* the royal seducer reveals his true identity, provides for the child he has fathered, and summons his courtiers to his side:

> He took the lassie in his arms
> And gae her kisses three

Book of Hours of James IV and Margaret Tudor.

David Allan. The
Gaberlunzie Man.

> And four and twenty hunder merk
> To pay the nurse's fee;
> He took a wee horn frae his side
> And blew baith loud and shrill
> And four and twenty belted knights
> Came skipping owre the hill.

In *The Gaberlunzie Man* the hero behaves like a bold Don Juan flirting
openly with a rustic maid before her mother's eyes, a scene
illustrated by David Allan in an etching published about 1800:

> He grew canty & and she grew fain.
> But little did her auld minny ken
> What thir slee twa together were saying
> Whan wooing they were sae thrang.

Long after James's death, stories of his wanderings and disguises
had passed into folk-memory, fact and legend woven together. The
printer of the poem *The Taill of Rauf Coilzear*, published in St
Andrews in 1572, almost certainly had James V in mind when he
decided to issue a Scottish version of this medieval Charlemagne

romance. A popular tale, it relates how Charlemagne takes refuge with a charcoal-burner, Rauf Coilzear, who, failing to recognize his guest's true identity, is later rewarded with honours. In real life James sometimes carried this play-acting too far, as when he travelled incognito through France in 1536 looking for a wife. What constructive purpose lay behind such irrational behaviour is difficult to discern but, as with a similar incident involving Joan of Arc a century earlier at the Dauphin's court at Chinon, the disguise was soon penetrated, and James was obliged to continue his journey as King of Scots and not as a humble royal servant. Despite this curious beginning his visit to France was a triumphant success and he returned to Scotland the following year with Madeleine, daughter of Francis I, as his bride. These royal pranks have inspired many a later poet both absurd and serious, from McGonagall to Scott, to spin tales about the 'poor man's king'.

A less attractive aspect of the king's character is revealed in the border ballad, *Johnnie Armstrong*, which tells of the merciless punishment meted out in 1530 to a border laird, John Armstrong of Gilnockie. This 'robber baron' had been defying the rule of law by running a system of protectionism in the district of Liddesdale. Lured by promises of safe conduct into a meeting with the king, he was seized and executed with a minimum of formality, despite repeated pleas for mercy. In the ballad James is portrayed in a very bad light and is shown as both vindictive and faithless. When Armstrong is led to execution he taunts the king with these words:

> To seek hot water beneath cold ice
> Surely it is a great follie.
> I have asked grace at a graceless face
> And there is none for my men and me.

This is the unacceptable face of James V, a far cry from the 'gudeman', but in keeping with the cruel severity of the monarch who condemned Lady Glamis to death by burning in 1537 on the Castle Hill of Edinburgh. The charge was treason, much disputed at the time and doubted since by some historians.

These flaws in the royal character were not apparent to every observer, and certainly not to the poet Ronsard, who knew the king personally and was in the entourage of James's first wife, Madeleine, when she came to Scotland in 1537. Ronsard, who is better known for his verses in praise of Mary Queen of Scots, was lavish in his admiration of her father, and his compliments were to be repeated a century later by another poet, William Drummond of Hawthornden, who also recorded some extravagant compliments by the Italian poet Ariosto. Ariosto, who knew the king only by report, chose Scotland as the setting for part of his *Orlando Furioso*, in which James appears as Zerbino, a prince 'of unexampled virtue and beauty rare'.

Quite apart from poems and legends about James V there is a strong tradition that he was something of a poet himself. Evidence that he wrote poetry comes from his lifelong friend and fellow poet, Sir David Lindsay of the Mount, who, as Master of the Royal Household during the king's minority, was not above reprimanding the young king for his sexual misbehaviour. The folk poem, *Christis Kirk on the Green,* is often attributed to James and certainly its subject matter – the deterioration of a rustic dance into something of an orgy – may not have been unfamiliar to him. By all accounts no Scottish monarch, before or since, was better qualified to describe at first hand scenes which bear more than a superficial resemblance to the ongoings in bawdy ballads of a later generation:

> Was never in Scotland heard nor seen
> Such dancing nor deray
> Neither in Falkland on the green
> Nor Peebles to the play,
> As was of wooers as I ween
> As Christis kirk on a day.

Poet or not, James V was certainly a serious patron of literature. In 1536 he appointed George Buchanan – the leading Scottish humanist of his day – tutor to his eldest bastard son, James, abbot of Kelso and Melrose. Buchanan, as a leading anti-clerical satirist, was also encouraged by the king to write two poems directed against the

Hector Boece. Hystory and croniklis of Scotland.

clergy, the *Palinodia* and the *Franciscanus*. Little did James realize in his eagerness to chastise the Church that, by employing Buchanan, he was nourishing the pen which would be responsible more than any other for destroying the reputation of his daughter Mary many years later. Another satirist who also enjoyed royal favour was Sir David Lindsay, who wrote in the vernacular and made a major contribution to the Scottish Reformation. His most popular work, the play *Ane Satyre of the Thrie Estaits*, was written probably at the instigation of the king himself and was first performed on Twelfth Night in 1540 at Linlithgow Palace before the entire court and several bishops. Castigating the sensuality and avarice of the clergy, the play seems to have made a strong first impression, for at the close of the performance the king summoned his bishops to his presence and delivered to them a stern lecture on the urgent need to reform the spiritual estate. Considering the notoriety of his private life it is not surprising that this advice fell mostly on deaf ears. Some reforms were indeed introduced, but it was a case of too little too late. The continued popularity of Lindsay's play in the years before the Reformation is indicative of a surprising degree of toleration in the Scottish court toward the sensitive question of religion. In 1554, fourteen years after its first performance, the play was put on at Greenside in Edinburgh in the presence of the Queen Regent, Mary of Guise, second wife of James V and mother of Mary Queen of Scots.

Fine Printing

The serious interest that James took in literature extended to printing and fine books, but a great deal probably perished in the burning of Edinburgh in 1544 during the Earl of Hertford's invasion, two years after the king's death. Very little in fact has survived from the royal library, apart from the manuscript of John Bellenden's *Chronicles of Scotland*, translated from the Latin of Hector Boece and bearing on its title-page the royal arms of Scotland and France. This book is now in the Pierpont Morgan Library in New York. Several payments relating to decorated manuscripts are recorded during the last years of James's reign (1538–42), possibly stimulated by his second marriage in June 1538 to Mary of Guise, an event which also coincided with a great increase in building activity at the royal palaces and castles. The richly decorated royal arms on the Cambuskenneth Cartulary of 1535 provides earlier evidence that this Augustinian abbey near Stirling was producing books for royal commission. About the same time, the King's Printer, Thomas Davidson, was producing fine work at his press in Edinburgh. In the last years of the reign, Davidson, by royal command, printed some of the best specimens of early Scottish typography known to survive – *The New Actis and Constitutionis of Parliament* (1541), elaborately illustrated with woodcuts; and Bellenden's translation of Hector Boece's *Hystory and croniklis of Scotland* (c.1536), widely admired for its excellent composition and splendid typeface.

Navigation

James V was not the only Stuart who possessed a great sense of style, but within an astonishingly short space of time and with limited resources he made a determined effort to bring the Scottish court onto a level with the splendours that he had witnessed during his visit to France in 1536–37. His interest in the visual arts was exceptional even for the Stuarts. This need to demonstrate royal power and magnificence was not, however, confined to the building of palaces with which he is most closely associated, but was also displayed in elaborate court festivities and in royal progresses up and down the country. The most extravagant of these journeys was his circumnavigation of Scotland in 1540, in a fleet of twelve ships that sailed from Leith to Dumbarton on a disciplinary exercise, enforcing law and order on the remoter coasts and islands of his kingdom. Travelling in great splendour the king occupied luxurious quarters on board, ate to the sound of music, and was served upon gold plate! Apart from its serious political purpose this royal progress was also of navigational value, for the pilot, Alexander Lindsay, made charts of the coastal waters, and kept detailed notes of the voyage. These were later translated into French by Nicholas de Nicolay, cosmographer to Henri II of France, and published in Paris in 1583 with the title *La navigation du Roy d'Escosse Iaques cinquiesme du nom autour de son royaume*. The map that this book contains is one of the earliest recognizable outlines of Scotland.

Architecture

Falkland Palace.

But above all else, James V was a great builder. The outburst of architectural activity in the last years of his reign was quite exceptional. It was undertaken on a scale never seen before or since in Scotland, and was unfortunately cut short by his early death in 1542, leaving many of his extravagant schemes unfinished. James was, of course, continuing the work begun in his father's reign when the great halls of Edinburgh and Stirling castles had been constructed and the palaces of Holyrood and Linlithgow began to take the shape that we know today. His visit to France in 1536 seems to have been the turning-point when his interest in architecture became something of an obsession. Having successfully accomplished his mission and returned home with a French wife and the renewal of 'the Auld Alliance', he immediately began to put into effect some of the ideas that he had imbibed at the French Court. The result was the planting on Scottish soil of a new architectural style, introducing French Renaissance details that were sharply different from those of the traditional Scottish castellated tower-houses of the period. The king supervised closely all that was going on as Holyrood, Stirling, Linlithgow and Falkland were transformed into centres of great activity with the designing of new façades, the introduction of Renaissance ornament and the importation of foreign craftsmen to work alongside Scottish masons. This development reached its peak in the years 1538–42 with the embellishment

Stirling Castle.

Palace of FALKLAND

The Prospect of Sterling Castle

of Falkland and the palace in Stirling Castle, the earliest surviving examples of Renaissance architecture in Britain. James saw himself as a truly modern man, a Renaissance prince fit to compete as a patron of the arts with his fellow monarchs in England and France. His grandiose building projects were the most ambitious ever undertaken by a Scottish monarch, and probably raised a few complaining eyebrows at the time, but the fact is that he had, within an astonishingly short space of time, transformed the architectural setting of the Scottish monarchy and provided a fitting backcloth against which the pageantry, masques, music and poetry of the Stuart court were to be enacted in the all too brief interludes that could be snatched from attending to the business of government. Court ceremonial in Scotland was prone to frequent disruption by political unrest or by long minorities. This meant that for long periods life at the court was conducted without the active supervision or participation of the reigning monarch. As a result, the architectural legacy that has been passed down is only a partial one, interrupted by the early death of its royal patron, damaged by the English invaders during the 'Rough Wooing' of the 1540s, and not greatly improved thereafter owing to the unrest during Mary's personal reign and the long minority of her son, James VI. Certain additions were made by James VI and Charles I, but it would be true to say that the credit for these royal buildings must go to James V who conceived, initiated and supervised their construction. Not until the reconstruction of Holyrood by Charles II after the Restoration was there another programme of royal building on a similar scale.

Such was the architectural transformation accomplished by James V that when his daughter Mary returned to Scotland in 1561 she would not have found herself, as is so often popularly supposed, in barbarous and unfamiliar surroundings; quite the reverse. For the palaces enlarged or rebuilt by her father only two decades before would still have been, for the most part, handsome in their newly-cut stone and painted interiors. She who had been reared in Renaissance châteaux would have found herself very much at home, albeit on a humbler scale, in Stirling, Linlithgow and Falkland where today some fine Renaissance workmanship still stands and where the spirit of the early Stuart court continues to breathe. Something of this spirit remains in the noble courtyard of Linlithgow with its elaborate fountain which so impressed Mary of Guise on her arrival from France in 1538; in the delicate classical buttresses and medallion busts on the façades at Falkland; and in the grotesque statuary on the palace in Stirling Castle which once shocked the prim Victorian architect Robert Billings, who condemned them as 'abominations' and 'obscene groups . . . betraying the fruits of an imagination luxuriant but revolting'.

The interiors of these buildings have fared less well, and not much now remains of their former splendour. The great hammer-beam roofs of the halls at Stirling and Linlithgow are now no more, vandalized by later insensitive hands or destroyed by criminal carelessness, a sorry record of Hanoverian neglect that provoked Robert Burns, in one of his less guarded moments, to protest:

> Here Stuarts once in triumph reigned
> And laws for Scotland's weal ordained,
> But now unroof'd their palace stands
> Their sceptre's sway'd by other hands.

Other parts of Scotland's royal heritage have been equally accident-prone, especially in the aftermath of the Jacobite risings in the 18th century when Linlithgow Palace was consumed by fire after being garrisoned by government troops, the Chapel Royal at Holyrood was allowed to fall into ruin, and, at Stirling, the great series of wooden medallions on the ceiling of the King's Presence Chamber were carelessly dismantled, dispersed, and partially destroyed. However, enough still remains in the painted decoration and carved woodwork of Mary's rooms at Holyrood and in the Chapel at Falkland to form some idea of the cultural ambience of the Stuart court during its short-lived Renaissance flowering. The present painstaking programme of restoration at Stirling Castle should, in time, reveal the long-hidden splendours of a noble sequence of palatial interiors constructed in the reigns of James IV and V and inhabited in their heyday by the courts of Queen Mary and her son James VI.

Death at Falkland

It was fitting that James V should end his short reign within the walls of one of his favourite palaces, at Falkland in December 1542, to which he had retired in despair and in a state of total mental collapse after his humiliating defeat on the Solway at the hands of an invading English army. His humiliation was compounded by the desertion of many of his nobles, a bitter contrast to the support which his father had commanded thirty years before at Flodden. James's subsequent death, while still an apparently healthy young man of no more than thirty, has never been satisfactorily explained, but at least he died in his bed unlike his father and daughter. The news of the latter's birth on December 8th at Linlithgow, instead of the hoped-for male heir, had been for him the final stroke of a malign fate, destroying his last vestige of hope and his will to live. In a moment of prophetic vision he appears to have foreseen that with her would perish the independence of the Scottish crown, and in essence his foreboding was to be proved correct. His legendary words – 'It cam wi' a lass and it will gang wi' a lass'* are among the foundation stones of the Stuart myth, a fitting opening to the sad tale of Mary, the most tragic figure in Stuart history.

---

*The exact form of the words supposedly said by James V on his deathbed has been disputed. In the 18th century David Hume preferred the anglicized version: 'The crown came with a woman'. In the 20th century the *Oxford Dictionary of Quotations* (1979) adds this fatuous comment: 'It is unlikely that James V spoke with a strong Scottish accent'!

Mary Stuart: the Many Faces of a Queen

Antipathy like flattery is the worst critic
Walter Sichel

It is no overstatement to say that Mary Queen of Scots is the best known and most controversial of all the Stuarts. Even today, at a distance of four centuries, her career, character, and reputation can arouse heated discussion in the most unexpected quarters, from the scholarly academic to the popular journalist. Few people having the slightest acquaintance with British and European history can contemplate her without prejudice, for not only does her life touch history at many levels – political, religious and cultural – but it also transcends history to reach the level of symbol and myth, and as such has become the favoured property of the poet and the artist. No firm consensus of opinion about her motives and character has been reached, nor is it ever likely to be, so she remains one of the most fascinating and notorious women in the pages of history, a fertile subject for endless speculation, fierce controversy, and all kinds of extravagant theorizing. In this way she continues to be a cultural force in a society where the political and religious issues that brought about her downfall have lost most, if not all, of their former power.

Unlike her forebears and successors on the Scottish throne, Mary did not exert a strong direct influence on the literary, artistic and scientific life of her times. Rarely a free agent, much of her brief personal reign in Scotland (1561–67) was absorbed in a desperate struggle for survival. Born to a virtually impossible task, which most of her Stuart predecessors and many of those who followed her were unable to master, she assumed personal responsibility for her bitterly divided kingdom at the age of eighteen, already widowed, separated from many of her subjects by her religion and upbringing in France, the first and only queen to rule Scotland in her own right. Her father on his deathbed had rightly guessed at her tragic destiny, a fate shared by many of her dynasty, though none to the same degree.

However, although Mary cannot be said to have exercised a profound cultural influence on the Scotland of her day, being neither a great builder like her father, nor a prolific writer like her son, her indirect influence was enormous. In the early years of her reign it was by inspiring creative writers that the youthful queen

Mary Stuart. Artist unknown.

39

exerted an influence on contemporary literature. Later, her life was to take a tragic and dramatic turn with the murder of Darnley and the events that followed, and it is the quality and extent of that personal tragedy which set her apart from almost every other royal figure in British history. It is this unique quality that has fascinated, and continues to enthrall, the historical and artistic imagination. In this respect, her influence has been, and still is, extraordinary and enduring.

The Youthful Queen

By all accounts Mary Stuart was a supremely cultivated woman. This was certainly the popular view in the early days of her reign. Even her most implacable foe, John Knox, admitted that she was a clever and formidable opponent. She seems to have made a strong impression on almost all who came into contact with her, softening the hostility of enemies and critics with her beauty and charm of manner, neither of which is always evident in contemporary portraits.

Mary shared to the full the Stuart love of poetry, and wrote some modest verses herself, but it is the poetry written in her honour that is remembered today. Her patronage of the leading French poets Pierre de Ronsard and Joachim du Bellay is well attested. Ronsard, the greatest of the Pléiade group of poets, knew her in her youth in France and later kept her portrait continually in front of him in his library. He compared her to the beauty of the dawn, addressing her as 'belle et plus que belle et agréable Aurore', and in his elegy on her departure for Scotland in August 1561 – surely one of the finest poems ever to be inspired by the Queen of Scots – he praises her in the manner of Petrarch addressing his beloved Laura:

> Like a beautiful meadow stripped of all its flowers,
> Like a painting of its colours all deprived,
> Like heaven void of all its myriad stars,
> Like a dry sea, a ship without a sail,
> A leafless woodland, cavern without gloom,
> A royal palace with no royal pomp,
> A ring having no priceless pearl inset –
> So shall France grieve at this her heavy loss,
> Her ornaments, and all her Royalty,
> Who was her colour, beauty, and her flower . . .

Du Bellay, for his part, likened her to Astraea who would usher in an age of gold, while a lesser but more notorious poet, Pierre de Chastelard, who accompanied Mary on her return to Scotland, allowed his poetic passion to affect his conduct to such a rash degree that he ended his days on the scaffold on a charge of compromising the queen's honour, the first but not the last of a long melancholy list of victims who died for Mary Stuart!

Pierre de Ronsard.   *George Buchanan.*

Within Scotland, she soon made a good impression, and in the early years of her reign won golden opinions in many quarters. The poet Alexander Scot welcomed her back with *Ane New Zeir Gift*, mixing conventional praise with thinly-veiled hints on how best to come to terms with the recently established Protestant Kirk:

> Welcum, illustrat Ladye, and oure Quene;
> Welcum oure lyone, with ye Floure-de-lyce;
> Welcum oure thrissill, with ye Lorane grene;
> Welcum oure rubent roiss vpoun ye ryce . . .

Of even greater weight were the praises of George Buchanan, the queen's secretary and one of Europe's foremost humanist poets. Although he was later to change his allegiance and become her fiercest critic, he was at this stage in his chequered career lavish with compliments: 'She was graced with surpassing loveliness of form, the vigour of maturing youth, and fine qualities of mind'. In his official capacity, Buchanan also wrote elegant Latin poems celebrating the elaborate court ceremonies in which the queen was involved, notably her marriage to the Dauphin in 1558 at Notre Dame in Paris, and later the masque at Stirling Castle in 1566 to celebrate the baptism of her son, the future James VI.

Sycophancy in court poets is perhaps only to be expected, but these glowing tributes are amply supported elsewhere in the reports of contemporaries. To many, her virtues and accomplishments – her love of poetry, history and music, her patronage of masques, her passion for dancing (so much deplored by Knox), her skill at embroidery, the splendour of her dress and jewels, the charm of her conversation both in Scots and in French and her wide knowledge of languages including Latin, Spanish and Italian – epitomized all that was considered desirable in a Renaissance princess. These attributes, combined with moderate political policies and a firm but

41

unfanatical religious faith that in retrospect seems remarkably tolerant for its time, paint a most favourable picture of the young Queen of Scots, the fair face of Mary Stuart one might say. Had she died before Darnley, this would have been the only face presented to posterity, and would have guaranteed for her a respectable but modest niche in history. In its general outlines it is a picture that fits the description of many a high-born Renaissance woman of the 16th century, and from what we know of Mary's education and her library she shared to the full the cultured tastes of the French court in which she was reared. In some ways it is a fairly conventional picture which gives no hint of what was to come. It hardly prepares us for the picture that emerges after the murder in 1567 of her second husband, Lord Darnley, when the seemingly serene goddess of Ronsard and Du Bellay is transformed into a distracted, tormented and apparently passionate woman lurching from one calamitous political mistake to another in a desperate effort to save her throne. From these tempestuous final years of her Scottish reign the legend of Mary Stuart is born, a legend that feeds upon the rapid and bewildering spiral of events that led from the murder of Darnley to the fatal Bothwell marriage, her subsequent imprisonment at Lochleven, abdication, flight into England, a long captivity of almost nineteen years, and finally, her trial and violent death. These turbulent events gave birth to the vast body of controversial literature that surrounds her name and continues to flow in an unceasing stream to this day. The questions that were asked then have continued to be raised with varying degrees of passion ever since. What exactly was her relationship with her Italian secretary David Rizzio? Did she connive at Darnley's murder? Was the Bothwell marriage freely entered into, or a desperate move forced upon her by dire necessity? Did she write the now long-lost Casket Letters? Why did she flee into England contrary to the advice of her supporters? What was her involvement in the Babington Plot and other conspiracies against Queen Elizabeth? Did she die a martyr's death, or was she just another Catholic politique?

Legends once born are apt to be carefully cultivated and jealously guarded, as if to preserve them from the cold prying eyes of historical research. In the case of Mary Stuart it is the legend and not the reality that tends to be uppermost in most minds, and this applies as much to certain historians as to poets and artists. Mary has become all things to all sorts of people, her character a blank sheet upon which generations of writers have left the imprint of their own prejudices and obsessions. Even the briefest glance at some of the literature written about her will astonish those who fondly imagine that the events of four centuries ago no longer have the power to arouse passions or to cloud the judgement of normally rational people. Some who embark upon this subject do so with a vindictive relish or a mendacious sentimentality that tells us far more about themselves than it can ever reveal about Mary Stuart. Only the reader can judge which pen is motivated by a zeal for truth or intoxicated with admiration for its own rhetoric.

The faces of the legend of Mary Stuart have divided not only historians and academics but equally poets, painters, novelists and dramatists. Attracted by a powerful blend of personal characteristics – physical beauty, royal rank, a disastrous marital history, alleged sexual misconduct and violent death – writers and artists have succumbed in large numbers to the magnetic fascination of this enigma, made all the more irresistible by the additional factor of religion.

Broadly speaking, there are four main schools of thought on Mary, 'the daughter of debate', as her rival Elizabeth described her. First, there is the 'more in sorrow than in anger' approach depicting Mary as a passionate, headstrong woman who sacrificed all for love and atoned for her sins on the scaffold in truly theatrical manner. This is a theory much beloved by novelists and all romantics. Second, the hardliners see her unequivocally as an adulteress and murderess, author of the Casket Letters, a relentless conspirator against England's Gloriana, and a deadly threat to the Protestant establishment; in all, a thoroughly dangerous woman who met her just deserts. These attitudes dominated the writing of most English historians until this century. A third point of view, mainly Catholic, paints a dramatically different picture of Mary as the Martyr Queen, betrayed by her countrymen and her son, abused and manipulated, grossly maligned and wrongfully imprisoned by a jealous rival, who had her put to death on account of her faith and her just right to the English throne. Less strongly held now than in previous centuries, this view has moderated its tone somewhat in these more ecumenical times and now prefers to see her as 'more sinned against than sinning'. Fourth, there is the increasingly popular 'no-nonsense' approach of some 20th-century writers who regard her as a foolish and hysterical woman, a fit subject for psychological study, but wholly unfitted for political power, a hopeless case whose importance has been greatly over-stressed and about whom far too much fuss has been made and much nonsense written. It is fascinating to trace these varying and radically differing interpretations in the writings of the learned, the famous, the obscure and the frankly scandal-mongering.

The Romantic Queen

If we look first at the popular romantic picture, it could be said that this is the most commonly held view even to the present day. The poems of Ronsard and du Bellay, and the admiring Latin verses of Buchanan – before disillusionment poisoned his pen – all paint a glowing picture of Mary in the days when fortune favoured her and the future seemed full of promise. Later, when scandal and tragedy had darkened her reputation, less emphasis was laid on her personal qualities, and she became for most of her contemporaries, and throughout the century that followed, a symbol of political and religious division. Not until the 18th century did the romantic aspect resurface and it has kept its hold ever since. Among the first to attempt her rehabilitation was the eccentric Walter Goodall, sub-librarian in the Advocates' Library in Edinburgh, and, for a time, assistant to the philosopher David Hume during the latter's brief term of office as Keeper of that Library. Goodall, or 'Watty' as he was affectionately known, had two great loves in his life: Mary Queen of Scots and the bottle. The latter may have affected his judgement of the former, and it may be wondered whether his romantic championship of her cause, and in particular his attempts to expose the Casket Letters as forgeries, did her reputation more harm than good. As an ardent Jacobite, Goodall, in his *Examination of the [Casket] Letters* (1754), warmly defended Mary's innocence of Darnley's murder, but Hume, who was not above teasing his assistant, was far less sympathetic, and took the view in his *History of England* that Mary was probably guilty. An amusing story is told of their rivalry in Chambers's *Eminent Scotsmen*. Entering the library one day, Hume found Goodall snoring over the manuscript of his treatise on Mary. Hume tiptoed up to his assistant and, laying his mouth to Watty's ear, roared out that 'Queen Mary was a whore, and had murdered her husband'. Watty stumbled to his feet and before he was properly awake sprang upon Hume, and seizing him by the throat, pushed him to the farther end of the library, exclaiming that he was 'some base Presbyterian parson, who was come to murder the character of Queen Mary, as his predecessors had contributed to murder her person'.

Other more illustrious champions were also prepared to take up the cudgels on Mary's behalf, notably that staunch English Tory and devout Anglican, Dr Samuel Johnson, on the occasion of his famous visit to Edinburgh in August 1773. Once more the calm of the Advocates' Library was shattered by a heated Marian controversy. Boswell in his *Journal of a Tour to the Hebrides* records Johnson's scornful comment when, during his visit to the library, the subject of Scotland's lost independence was raised: 'Sir, never talk of your independency, who could let your Queen remain twenty years in captivity and then be put to death without even a pretence of justice, without your ever attempting to rescue her; and such a Queen, too! – as every man of any gallantry of spirit would have sacrificed his life for.' Worthy Mr. James Ker, Keeper of the Records: 'Half our nation was bribed by English money.' Johnson: 'Sir, that is no defence; that makes you worse.' Good Mr. Brown, Keeper of the Advocates' Library: 'We had better say nothing about it.' This spirited defence of Mary is not unlike a similar chivalrous outburst twenty years later by the Irish orator Edmund Burke on behalf of the doomed Marie Antoinette, whose life and tragic end are in some respects similar to that of the Queen of Scots. 'I thought ten thousand swords must have leaped from their scabbards to avenge even a look that threatened her with insult. But the age of chivalry is gone.'

Mary's defenders were not only to be found in the ranks of literary men. A champion of a very different kind, the Methodist preacher John Wesley, records in his *Journal* a visit to Holyrood in 1761 during which he pauses before a portrait of the queen and reflects 'It is scarce possible for any who looks at this, to think her such a monster as some have painted her; nor indeed for any who considers the circumstances of her death, equal to that of an ancient martyr'. On another occasion, after reading Goodall's defence of Mary, Wesley accuses Buchanan of throwing dirt at his former benefactress and compares Queen Elizabeth to Nero! But to return to the poets. Surely few have caught the melancholy hopelessness and bitter resignation of her long captivity better than Scotland's own national bard Robert Burns in his *Lament of Mary Queen of Scots on the Approach of Spring*:

> I was the Queen o'bonie France,
> Where happy I hae been;
> Fu' lightly rase I on the morn,
> As blythe lay down at e'en:
> And I'm the sovereign of Scotland,
> And mony a traitor there;
> Yet here I lie in foreign bands,
> And never ending care.

Scarcely less haunting is the underlying thread of doom and menace that James Hogg (the 'Ettrick Shepherd') weaves through the introduction to his long poem, *The Queen's Wake*:

> Though courtiers fawned and ladies sung,
> Still in her ear the accents rung, –
> 'Watch thy young bosom and maiden eye,
> For the shower must fall and the flowret die'.

A lighter touch is provided by the child poet Marjory Fleming who added her tears to those of her elders in the following charming lines:

> Queen Mary was much loved by all,
> Both by the great and by the small,
> But hark! her soul to heaven doth rise!
> And I suppose she has gained a prize –
> For I do think she would not go
> Into the awful place below.

To the writers and composers of the Romantic Revival the subject of Mary Stuart was ideally suited. In the late 18th and early 19th centuries her name figures prominently in European literature. Two of the major dramatists of the time, the Italian, Vittorio Alfieri (also well known for his liaison with the last Stuart queen, Louise of Stolberg, the estranged wife of Bonnie Prince Charlie), and the German, Friedrich Schiller, both wrote plays about Mary. Schiller's powerful *Maria Stuart* of 1801 is still widely performed, the translation by Stephen Spender being particularly moving. His play inspired Donizetti's opera, *Maria Stuarda*, a work which reaches its climax in the dramatic although fictional encounter between the two rival queens, Mary and Elizabeth. The composer Schumann also wrote sorrowful lieder around the theme of the Queen of Scots. The list of plays, operas, ballets, songs and overtures is endless, and shows no sign of abating in the late 20th century. Overwhelmingly, the treatment is personal and romantic, ranging from the sublime to the absurd. Few are of the quality of Schiller's tragedy, and most are rarely performed today. At one end of the scale are dramatic works by Swinburne, Drinkwater, and Björnson, and at the other some particularly unfortunate attempts by the cinema industry to portray Mary on the screen.

In the genre of the novel, the public appetite for historical romance continues to be insatiable, and few stories can match or surpass this one. Since the days of Sir Walter Scott whose portrayal of the imprisoned queen at Lochleven Castle in *The Abbot* has rarely been bettered in prose – 'Who is there, that, at the very mention of Mary Stewart's name, has not her countenance before him, familiar as that of the mistress of his youth, or the favourite daughter of his advanced age?' – a relentless stream of fiction both good and bad has provided trade for publishers and booksellers and solace for countless readers. The pens of Alexandre Dumas, Carola Oman, Margaret Irwin and Hugh Walpole, to name but a few, have worked this rich vein of inspiration which continues to show no sign of exhaustion. However, whenever her name needs a defender it is the poets whose lines linger most in the memory. Less firm and dogmatic than prose, poetry can capture the elusive quality that envelops the enigma of Mary Stuart. Her tragic end has given her a kind of romantic immortality; in the words of Boris Pasternak as translated by Michael Harari,

> Her death's heroic; this keeps her at her prime,
> Wraps her in rumour; she's the talk of time.

Or, as Alan Bold, writing in 1985, puts it:

> Mary Stuart
> Ye broke the hert
> O mony mony men
> An' ye'd a frosty pow
> An' a sair-sunk brow
> Afore they killed ye, hen;
> The axe hacked thrice
> An' ye caa'd tae Christ
> That Wednesday at ten
> An' I'll aywis see
> Till ma country's free
> Them murder ye again.

The Wicked Queen

The second face of Mary Stuart, that of the dangerous intriguer, the adulteress and murderess, is one interpretation that still commands wide support, although less vehemently argued now than in the past. It is an image that is more often found in print than painted on canvas, pictorial representations being generally more favourable to the queen's character if not to her beauty. At its more moderate level it represents a consistent thread of thinking in English historical writing from the 16th to the 20th centuries. The biographical entry under her name in *The Dictionary of National Biography* is typical of this school of thought, which, with varying degrees of censoriousness, can be found in the pages of David Hume, William Robertson, and David Hay Fleming, to name some of the most eminent. Their view is that she was a ruler who, although possessed of some good qualities, behaved at moments of crisis with a dangerous and passionate irresponsibility, and allied herself with political and religious forces that were profoundly hostile to the true interests of the majority of her countrymen.

This approach has the virtue, not always shared by that of the romantics, of perceiving that Mary was a deadly menace to the political establishment of her day, and that her actions threatened incalculable consequences for the future stability of both Scotland and England. Like Jacobitism in the 18th century, she was a political problem of supreme importance, a dilemma which only her death could resolve. From the first days of her return to Scotland some of the keener observers immediately recognized this threat, and none more clearly than John Knox. No sooner had she set foot on Scottish soil than the Reformer made this pronouncement in typically Biblical fashion: 'The very face of heaven, the time of her arrival, did manifestly speak what comfort was brought unto this country with her, to wit, sorrow, dolour, darkness, and all impiety'. In his *History of the Reformation in Scotland*, he uses much stronger language, comparing her to Jezebel and Athaliah, accusing her of whoredom and worse, 'for greater abomination was never in the nature of any woman than is in her, whereof we have but seen only the buds; but we will after taste of the ripe fruit of her impiety, if God cut not her days short'. The language is not unlike that which he had employed against Mary's mother, Mary of Guise, a ruler who has generally been viewed much more favourably, but Knox found no difficulty in transferring his loathing of the mother to the daughter.

Knox at least has the virtue of consistency, unlike Mary's secretary George Buchanan, who swung from extravagant praise to fabricated vilification. To Knox as author of the anti-feminist tract, *The First Blast of the Trumpet against the Monstruous Regiment of Women*, Mary Stuart as a ruler was trebly repugnant on account of her femininity, her Catholic faith, and her French connexions; but he did not make the mistake of underestimating her intelligence and power as a dangerous opponent: 'If there be not in her . . . a proud mind, a crafty wit, and an indurate heart against God and his truth, my judgment faileth me'. Buchanan also pays tribute to her cleverness in his *Rerum Scoticarum Historia*, drawing attention to 'fine qualities of mind' which, he adds ominously, were 'made more attractive by a surface gloss of virtue'. For more than a century after

John Knox.

Mary's death it was Buchanan's damning indictment of her conduct in *Ane Detectioun of the duinges of Marie Quene of Scottes, touchand the murder of hir husband, and hir conspiracie, adulterie, and pretensed mariage with the Erle Bothwell* that mostly influenced opinion in the Protestant countries of Europe, and not the denunciations of Knox. Later, however, in the early 18th century, the meticulous scholarship of Thomas Ruddiman, the Keeper of the Advocates' Library, and of Father Thomas Innes of the Scots College in Paris exposed the grave inadequacies of Buchanan as a reliable historian. It is now widely agreed that his history is untrustworthy as an account of Mary's personal reign, being based upon insinuation, half-truth, and blatant falsehood, all inextricably woven together.

As a chief exponent of the principles of anti-monarchism and as a great Latin stylist, Buchanan dominated much of the political thinking of the 17th and 18th centuries during the struggles between the Stuarts and their opponents. Against this background of political upheaval the accuracy of his case against Mary was considered less important than the validity or otherwise of his views as a political theorist. In this unfavourable climate the defenders of the queen had a hard struggle to make their voices heard – far less respected – and it was not until the more temperate judgements of David Hume and William Robertson in the mid-18th century that these controversies received more dispassionate treatment. Hume, after praising Mary as 'a princess of great accomplishments both of body and mind, natural as well as acquired', finds it difficult – as others have done before and since – to reconcile these fine qualities with some of her actions, and concludes severely that 'an enumeration of her qualities might carry the appearance of a panegyric; an account of her conduct must, in some parts, wear the aspect of a severe satire and invective'. The less censorious Robertson admitted to being baffled in his attempt to paint a convincing picture of her from radically conflicting accounts, and satisfied himself with a fairly non-committal opinion on the merits of the two opposing schools of thought: 'She neither merited the exaggerated praises of the one, nor the undistinguishing censure of the other'. This strain of paternalistic forbearance did not long outlast the demise of the leaders of the Enlightenment, and with the revival of religious feeling in the 19th century the old refrain of sectarian rhetoric re-asserted itself. The distorting effects of religious sectarianism, which make it so difficult to reach any consensus of opinion or to form a true and convincing picture of Mary from the writings of 16th- and 17th-century writers, re-emerge in some of the great authors of Victorian prose. The striving for some degree of historical objectivity by the earlier historians of the Enlightenment is in stark contrast to the triumphant passages of passionate prose indulged in by such as James Anthony Froude and Thomas Carlyle. No more serious charges against her have ever been made than those contained in Froude's *History of England*. Torn between admiration for her courage on the scaffold and contempt for all that she represented he pronounces:

> Never did any human creature meet death more bravely; yet, in the midst of the admiration and pity which cannot be refused her, it is not to be forgotten that she was leaving the world with a lie upon her lips. She was a bad woman, disguised in the livery of a martyr.

And then he adds a stinging comment on attempts by her co-religionists in his own day to invest her memory with an aura of martyrdom:

> She could not, indeed, stay the progress of the Reformation, make England a province of Spain, or arrest the dissolution of an exploded creed; but she became a fitting tutelary saint for the sentimental Romanism of the modern world.

In slightly less vitriolic mood, Thomas Carlyle, in his *Historical Sketches*, concedes that she had her good points, but detects in her a dash of the gypsy, something that seems to have escaped the notice of other writers:

> A high kind of woman; with haughty energies, most flashing, fitful discernments, generosities; too fitful all, though most gracefully elaborated: the born daughter of heroes, – but sore

involved in Papistries, French coquetries, poor woman: and had the dash of Gypsy tragic in her, I doubt not; and was seductive enough to several, instead of being divinely beautiful to all.

Again, in his essay, *The Portraits of John Knox*, Carlyle compares her to Medea and Clytemnestra, but at the same time seems to sense the impossibility of her destiny and the 'chaos of contradictions' in her nature, concluding with apparent even-handedness:

> Alas, she meant no harm to Scotland; was perhaps loyally wishing the reverse; but was she not with her whole industry doing, or endeavouring to do, the sum-total of all harm whatsoever that was possible for Scotland, namely the covering it up in Papist darkness, as in an accursed winding-sheet of spiritual death eternal?

This is a far cry from the kind of history to which the modern reader is accustomed; very different from the restraint of Hume and Robertson; and more akin to the writers of the 16th century, the age of Knox and deep religious conviction.

However, if the language of Froude and Carlyle seems strong, it pales beside the high tone of moral indignation that pervades the pages of that immensely popular and influential Victorian novel, *Westward Ho!* whose author, Charles Kingsley, the apostle of Christian Socialism and 'muscular' Christianity, gave expression in his books to some of the deepest feelings of his countrymen at a time when the British Empire was at its height. As a novel, it kept its popularity with generations of schoolboys well into this century, but what concerns us here is his portrayal of Mary. When the news of her execution at Fotheringhay is made public his pen quivers with emotion as he describes the joyful reactions of the English people:

> All England, like a dreamer who shakes off some hideous nightmare, has leapt up in one tremendous shout of jubilation, as the terror and the danger of seventeen anxious years is lifted from its heart for ever.

He goes on to lecture his reader on the alleged vices of the Queen of Scots:

> And now she can do evil no more. Murder and adultery, the heart which knew no forgiveness, the tongue which could not speak truth even for its own interest, have past and are perhaps atoned for; and her fair face hangs a pitiful dream in the memory even of those who knew that either she or England must perish.

Warming to his task, he adds,

> Of her the Jesuits were not unmindful; and found it convenient, indeed to forget awhile the sorrows of the Queen of Heaven in those of the Queen of Scots. Not that they cared much for those sorrows; but they were an excellent stock-in-trade. She was a Romanist; she was 'beautiful and unfortunate', a virtue which, like charity, hides the multitude of sins.

Kingsley concludes with this astonishing volte-face: 'Into her merits or demerits I do not enter deeply here. Let her rest in peace'.

The influence of such views in vigorous prose, surely more scarlet than purple, was incalculable in an age of imperialism when religious and nationalist controversies were at their fiercest. To such as Froude and Kingsley the most intolerable aspect of Mary Stuart's story was, one suspects, the heroic manner of her death with its strong religious overtones. Kingsley's is only the most extreme example of a particular point of view, and should be seen in the context and against the background of a religious, political and literary battle that was going on in Victorian England over such burning issues as the restoration of the English Roman Catholic Hierarchy, papal claims of infallibility, and the convening of the first Vatican Council in 1870. This was a struggle in which Kingsley himself became involved when he turned from the writing of fiction to attack John Henry Newman in print. In this heated climate the cause of Mary Stuart acquired a new relevance and immediacy. Attempts by some in the archdiocese of Westminster to have her beatified as a martyr on the occasion of her tercentenary in 1887 were not calculated to cool sectarian tempers. Today, those who take a strong anti-Marian line do so from a rather different standpoint, but although religious passions have cooled, the tone of moral disapproval is still evident in, for example, Edith Sitwell's *The Queens and the Hive*, and George Malcolm Thomson's *The Crime of Mary Stuart*.

From the ranks of the poets also the adversaries of Mary claim support. Some of the greatest names in English literature have worked on this theme, notably her contemporary, Edmund Spenser, in whose allegory, *The Faerie Queene*, she appears under various guises as Duessa and Radegund, but always in a sinister light. In Book V Canto VII the duel between Radegund and Britomart is clearly intended to represent the conflict between Mary and Elizabeth. Shakespeare, whose life spans the execution of Mary, the death of Elizabeth, and her replacement on the throne by Mary's son, could no doubt have written, had he dared, a splendid tragedy around these themes. The terrible irony of the situation could not have escaped him, and has indeed spurred some commentators to suggest that he wrote *Hamlet* with this theme in mind. The Cambridge dramatist, James Plumptre, makes this very point in his *Observations on Hamlet . . . as an indirect censure on Mary Queen of Scots* (1796), claiming that the marriage of Hamlet's mother,

Queen Gertrude, to Claudius, the murderer of her first husband, is modelled on that of Mary to Bothwell. Much ink has been spilt on this intriguing theory. Others, including the Austrian Stefan Zweig, find strong parallels between *Macbeth, King Lear*, and events in Mary's life. These are all examples of the extent to which her story has become the property of every kind of theorist and speculator, a bottomless well of inspiration from which can be drawn ideas to please every taste and to quench the thirst of the most devoted Marianist.

The poets and dramatists of the present day, while not uncritical, are, with the passage of four centuries, more inclined to make allowances and to see her tragedy in personal rather than dynastic or sectarian terms. Her portrayal in the modern dramas of Robert Bolt and Robert Kemp shows some sympathy for her plight even when the general approach is antipathetic. Rebuke in the beautiful poem, *Alas, Poor Queen*, by Marion Angus, is balanced by pity:

> Consider the way she had to go,
> Think of the hungry snare,
> The net she herself had woven,
> Aware or unaware,
> Of the dancing feet grown still,
> The blinded eyes –

but the avenging tones of the Old Testament can still be heard in *John Knox*, by Iain Crichton Smith:

> A thunderous God tolls from a northern sky.
> He pulls the clouds like bandages awry.
> See how the harlot bleeds below her crown. . . .
> The shearing naked absolute blade has torn
> through false French roses to her foreign cry.

The Martyr Queen

In stark contrast, and indeed so different that it would seem to belong to another person altogether, the third face of Mary Stuart, that of the wronged woman, the innocent victim and martyr, is still held up before the judgement of the world as a true image. It is found mostly in the pages of Catholic apologists or on canvas, but occasionally an advocate will be found who is brave or foolhardy enough to cross the sectarian or political boundaries of his or her cultural background to plead before the bar of public opinion on behalf of the Queen of Scots. In depth of passion and range of invective her defenders yield nothing to the other side, and here, as elsewhere, the arguments vary from the reasonable to the absurd. As one historian pointed out in *Essays on the Scottish Reformation* (1962), Mary's conduct after the murder of Darnley would have had few defenders had it not been for her twenty years in prison and the heroic manner of her death. This is the part of her life that provides the basis for the vast literature of martyrdom that flooded Europe in the century following her execution, a flood that continued with reduced fervour into the 18th century, took a fresh lease of life in the 19th century, and is still revived from time to time in an age largely indifferent to questions of sanctity and holiness. As with the opposing school of thought, it has suffered in this century from the decline of public interest in the issues of the Reformation, and much of what was said and written now seems to be of little more than academic interest.

Naturally, Mary has retained a special place in the affections of Scottish Catholics, not only because she was the last Catholic sovereign to rule over the independent kingdom of Scotland, but also on account of her patronage of the Scots Colleges at Paris and Douai which were both active after the Reformation as seminaries training priests for the missions at home. In the famous and near-contemporary 'memorial portrait' of her at Blairs College, close to

see plates page 5

Aberdeen, she is described as foundress of the College at Douai, and in the magnificently illustrated *Book of Grisy*, the cartulary of the Scots College in Paris, Mary is portrayed receiving petitions from poor students to whom she is known to have responded from her own financial reserves during her imprisonment. The figures and accompanying verses in this beautiful manuscript are composed with great skill and artistry, a precious survival of the art of the French Renaissance. Another Catholic memento of Mary is the

Book of Grisy.

see plates page 6

Blairs Jewel which contains a miniature portrait of her, thought to have been painted from life between 1575 and 1580, mounted as a reliquary and bearing on the frame the names of Catholic martyrs.

Mary the Martyr Queen was as popular with the artist and engraver as with the literary propagandist and dramatist, and it is in the 'memorial portrait' at Blairs College that her apotheosis is most vividly depicted. This painting, whose escape from destruction in the Scots College at Douai during the French Revolution is in itself an exciting tale, depicts her as a martyr for the Catholic faith, bearing the symbols of that faith on the scaffold, and displaying the regal serenity and courage that is confirmed by all contemporary accounts of her death. With varying degrees of accuracy and fervour this image dominated most Catholic and much of European writing for centuries. Reliable accounts of every detail of her last hours at Fotheringhay have survived, and, despite the attempts of the Elizabethan government to suppress information, the story was soon on the presses of the printing-houses of Europe. Strong parallels exist between the horrified reactions to her death and those that followed upon the execution of her grandson, Charles I, at Whitehall in 1649. Both monarchs suffered a similar fate for a variety of political and religious reasons after undergoing long periods of imprisonment ending in their arraignment before quasi-judicial proceedings of dubious legality that shocked contemporary Europe. The assassination or deposition of monarchs was not uncommon in European history, but official trial followed by public execution was

proteste de la recepvoir innocente de tout crime quant je serois leur subiecte la religion catolique & le maintien du droit que dieu m'a donné à ceste couronne sont les deux poincts de ma condampnation & toutesfoys ilz ne me veulent permettre de dire que c'est pour la religion catolique que je meurs mays pour la crainte du change de la leur & pour preuve ilz m'ont osté mon aumosnier lequel bien qu'il soit en la mayson je n'ay peu obtenir qu'il me vinst confesser ny communier à ma mort mays m'ont faict grande instance de recepvoir la consolation & doctrine de leur ministre amené pour ce faict ce porteur & sa compagnie la pluspart de vos subiectz vous tesmoigneront mes desportemantz en ce mien acte dernier il reste que je vous suplie comme Roy tres Chrestien mon beau frere & ancien allyé & qui m'avez tousiours protesté de m'aymer qu'a ce coup vous faysiez preuve en tous ces poinctz de vostre vertu tant par charité me soulageant de ce que pour descharger ma conscience je ne puis sans vous qui est de recompenser mes serviteurs desolez leur laissant leurs gages l'autre faysant prier dieu pour une royne qui a esté nommée tres Chrestienne & meurt catolique desnuée de tous ses biens quant à mon filz je le vous recommande autant qu'il le meritera car je n'en puis respondre j'ay pris la hardiesse de vous envoier deux pierres rares pour la santé vous la desirant parfaicte avec heureuse & longue vie vous les recevrez comme de vostre tres affectionnée belle soeur mourante en vous rendant tesmoignage de son bon cueur envers vous je vous recommande encores mes serviteurs vous ordonnerez si il vous plaict que pour mon ame je soye payée de partye de ce que me debvez & qu'en l'honneur de Jhesus Christ lequel je prieray demain à ma mort pour vous me laysser de quoy fonder un obit & faire les aumosnes requises ce mercredy a deux heures apres minuit

Vostre tres affectionnée et bien bonne soeur MarieR

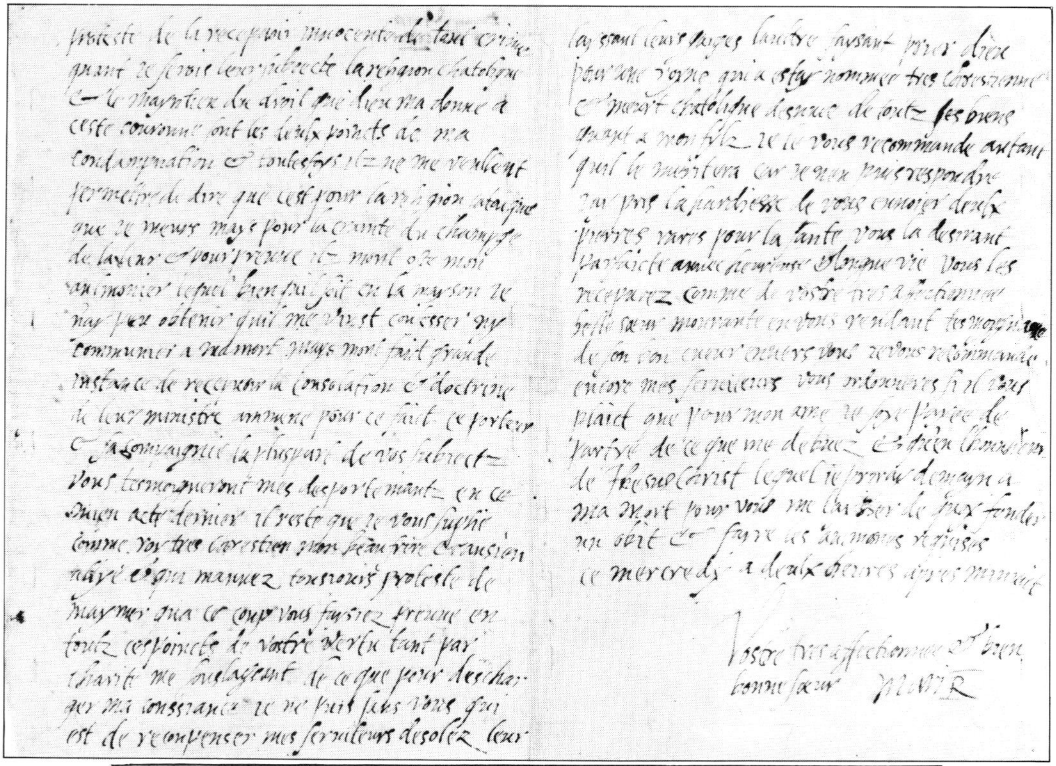

Mary's Last Letter.

quite another matter, and the literature of protest that these events provoked soon grew into a torrent. The glorification of King Charles is popularly linked with one book only, the *Eikon Basilike*; Mary's case is very different: a multitude of defenders pursuing her enemies in print and on canvas with a zeal that the passage of centuries did little to abate.

Among her earliest and most ardent supporters were John Lesley, Bishop of Ross, the judge and historian David Chambers, and Adam Blackwood, author of *Martyre de la royne d'Escosse*, all leaders in a campaign to vindicate her honour and redeem her reputation. None, however, seems to have caught the imagination of the reading public with quite the same force as Knox and Buchanan, the chief architects of the case for the prosecution. More eloquent in her own defence are the words of Mary herself in the famous last letter written to her brother-in-law Henri III of France on the eve of her execution. The tone of sorrowful resignation is evident, but does not obliterate her conviction in the justice of her own cause:

> Thanks be to God, I scorn death and vow that I meet it innocent of any crime, even if I were their subject. The Catholic faith and the assertion of my God-given right to the English crown are the two issues on which I am condemned.

Her choice of words is quiet, restrained and dignified, as was her conduct a few hours later on the scaffold. It would be difficult not to feel some emotion in reading this historic document which, like much that is associated with its author, has had an exciting history. Passing eventually from royal ownership into the archives of the Scots College in Paris, it remained there until the French Revolution, when, in the company of other precious manuscripts, it vanished from sight for a time before passing into private ownership and ultimately in this century to the National Library in Edinburgh, where it is now one of the principal treasures. It is not the only manuscript in Mary's hand that has survived from her captivity, for apart from volumes of her letters edited by Prince Labanoff and published in 1844, there is her doleful *Essay on Adversity*, which was composed in French and reveals a reflective cast of mind very different from that of the impulsive young ruler of Scotland two decades earlier. Her sentiments are phrased in the language of conventional Christian piety, as were the meticulous preparations that she made for her death when that finally had to be faced – the careful choice of dress, the crucifix, the rosary beads, the prayer book – all in keeping with the air of apparent unconcern and calm that she displayed in the great hall of Fotheringhay Castle on February 8th 1587. From what history has told us of the events of that fateful morning, Mary was the most composed and cheerful person present, seemingly eager to be free of an existence that had long proved intolerable. Not so the executioner, who, unnerved by the dreadful tension of the moment, had to wield his axe three times before the head of Mary Stuart finally fell.

Her behaviour during those final moments was greatly admired at the time by friend and foe alike, but has since been criticized for an element of theatricality by those who detect in it the last vain gestures of a dangerous enchantress. Understandably, her supporters – including some of those who had been less than vocal in her support while she lived – seized upon it to sing her praises in prose, in sermons, in poetry, in drama and in paint. Whether or not she wrote the following poetic affirmation of faith on the morning of her execution is not absolutely certain, but it is commonly attributed to her:

> O Domine Deus! speravi in te.
> O care mi Jesu, nunc libera me!
> In dura catena, in misera poena, desidero
> Languendo, gemendo, et genu flectendo,
> Adoro, imploro, ut liberes me.

During her trial, a few months before, she had warned her judges to 'remember that the theatre of the world is wider than the realm of England', and her prophecy was proved correct by the wave of moral indignation that was directed at Elizabeth and her advisers when details of the execution became known.

Nowhere was the rhetoric more fiery than in the sermon that was delivered at a Requiem Mass before the French court on 12 March 1587 in the black-draped cathedral of Notre Dame in Paris. The preacher on that occasion was Renaud de Beaune, Archbishop of Bourges, who was old enough to remember the day nearly thirty years before when Mary had been married to the Dauphin in the self-same cathedral. Commenting at length on the poignant contrast

Verstegan. Théâtre des Cruautez. 1588.

between these two great events, the preacher concluded: 'Oh vanity of human greatness, shall we never be convinced of your deceitfulness'. This sermon was printed in Paris the following year bearing a title that castigates the English as heretics and enemies of God. Throughout France there were demonstrations virtually canonizing Mary as a martyr for her faith; in Spain preparations for the Armada were given fresh impetus by her death; while in Scotland the sense of humiliation and anger felt by ordinary people was in strong contrast to the timid ambivalence of Mary's own son, James VI. Patriotic poems and posters circulated in the streets of Edinburgh condemning 'Jezabel that English whore . . . for murdering our Queen', but the King of Scots, with his eye on the English crown and no doubt fearing another Flodden, was prepared to swallow the insult to his family and his nation. Not until he was safely on the throne of England sixteen years later did James belatedly take steps to do his filial duty by ordering his mother's remains to be transferred to Westminster Abbey, where a magnificent monument and effigy were erected in uncomfortable proximity to the tomb of Elizabeth. James went further, and instructed the English historian William Camden to refute in print the errors and libels of George Buchanan, who, as tutor to the young King of Scots, had so manifestly failed to inculcate into his royal pupil a proper appreciation of his mother's wicked ways!

Less politically motivated were the lyrics that flowed from the pens of poets such as the English Jesuit Robert Southwell, whose *Decease, Release*, written shortly after Mary's execution, accurately prophesied the continuance of her power and fascination after death:

David Allan. Murder of Rizzio.

Alive a Queene, now dead I am a Sainte,
Once Mary calld, my name nowe Martyr is,
From earthly raigne debarred by restraint,
In liew whereof I raigne in heavenly blisse.

Another poet who hailed her death as a martyrdom was a young Italian, Maffeo Barberini, the future Pope Urban VIII, who composed *De Nece Reginae Scotiae* in her honour. This youthful gesture was not forgotten when many years later, in 1624, the Aberdonian George Conn dedicated his life of Mary to the Barberini Pope. Also dedicated to Urban VIII was a poem on her by the Spanish dramatist Lope de Vega entitled *Corona Tragica. Vida y muerte de la Reyna de Escocia*, published in Madrid in 1627. The list is interminable, and illustrates the intermingling of genuine Christian piety with political calculation that was so characteristic of European religious literature in the era of the Reformation and the Counter-Reformation.

At home, Mary's cause became not only a rallying cry for persecuted Catholics in 17th-century Britain, but also a useful symbol for the Stuart monarchy in its long struggles with parliament and the puritans. Numerous engravings of Mary as martyr and heroine feature as frontispieces and in the text of printed books of the period, among them Sir William Sanderson's *Compleat History of Mary Queen of Scotland* (1656), and Pierre Le Moyne's *Gallery of Heroick Women* (1652). Some earlier works, like Verstegan's *Théâtre des Cruautez* (1588), depict the actual execution in grim detail; others, at a later date, choose to show her in a variety of unlikely and affected poses more suited to the stage than to real life. As the 18th century advanced and religious fervour diminished, artists and engravers begin to see her in a different light. The David Allan

W. N. Gardiner.
Mary kneeling before
her executioner.

Pittendrigh Macgillivray. Maria Regina Scotorum.

drawings in the National Gallery of Scotland give her an almost doll-like appearance, as if she were merely a puppet in a historical pageant. Engravings by William Nelson Gardiner published in 1791 to music by Willoughby Bertie, 4th Lord Abingdon, portray her as a figure from contemporary fashionable society, not unlike Nelson's Emma Hamilton in one of her famous 'attitudes'. Artistic licence in the service of political or religious propaganda is not of course confined to any one period in history, but by the middle of the 19th century a more serious approach toward historical accuracy is discernible, and one that is more in keeping with its subject. As the tercentenary of Mary's execution came near, historians and artists alike rekindled public interest in the vexed question of martyrdom. The lawyer, John Hosack, vigorously defended her in his *Mary Queen of Scots and Her Accusers* (1869), describing her in his closing paragraph as 'this illustrious victim of sectarian violence and barbarous statecraft'. A German writer, Dr Bernhard Sepp, published several works in Munich in the 1880s, vindicating her cause, as did Victor Canet, professor of history at Lille, in his *Marie Stuart, la Reine Martyre* (1892). Among a host of similar titles, one of the most interesting came from the pen of an elder in the Church of Scotland who chose to remain anonymous. His *Mary Queen of Scots. A Narrative and Defence* (1889) is dedicated to her memory as Martyr Queen. The same strongly sympathetic treatment is evident in *The Tragedy of Fotheringay* (1895), by Mrs Maxwell Scott of Abbotsford and in Sir Edward Parry's *Persecution of Mary Stewart* (1931). Less well known is a portrait of Mary by the Scottish artist and poet, Pittendrigh Macgillivray, in the Spring 1895 issue of *The Evergreen*. Here she is shown in a triumphant – almost defiant – pose, as if conscious of her impending martyrdom and facing it with unflinching determination. The artist has probably taken his inspiration from the Douai 'memorial' portrait of three centuries before.

The verdict of the Catholic Church on Mary Stuart has been conspicuously more cautious than that of the writer and artist. In the early years after her death, the widespread popular acclaim that spread throughout Catholic Europe was not reflected in official ecclesiastical pronouncements, and although the question of her beatification was raised during the pontificate of Benedict XIV in the middle of the 18th century, no firm action was taken. Later, during the French Revolution, Pope Pius VI compared the heroism and piety of her end to that of Louis XVI, but beyond that the papacy was not prepared to venture. On the occasion of her tercentenary in 1887 the question was raised once again by the recently restored English Catholic hierarchy under the direction of Cardinal Manning of Westminster. Rome, however, remained unconvinced, and there the matter has remained ever since. In this highly controversial area the Church has chosen to adopt the old Scots legal verdict of 'not proven'.

The Foolish Queen

The fourth face of Mary Stuart, that of the foolish and hysterical woman unfitted for the responsibilities of high office, is one that has gained increasing acceptance this century, although hinted at by earlier writers. Much 20th-century literature, with its suspicion of political ideals, and scepticism about religious beliefs, has little sympathy with either of the two opposing schools of Marianist polemics. Equally, many writers of today are unmoved by the theories of the romanticists. At worst, this attitude of disenchantment appeals to a popular taste for the anti-hero, for detraction and salacious gossip. At best, it is a healthy reaction against the overheated prose of the past. Curiously it was John Knox who struck the first blow against Mary's fitness to rule even before her return to

Scotland in 1561, for although not aimed directly at her, his now famous *The First Blast of the Trumpet against the Monstruous Regiment of Women*, published in Geneva in 1558, declaimed in thunderous prose against all feminine rule:

> To promote a woman to bear rule, superiority, dominion or empire above any realm, nation, or city, is repugnant to nature, contumely to God, a thing most contrarious to his revealed will and approved ordinance, and finally it is the subversion of good order, of all equity and justice.

When he wrote these historic words, Knox had in mind Mary Tudor in England and Mary of Guise in Scotland, but the subsequent history of the detested Mary Stuart must have seemed to him a clear vindication of the arguments put forward in his book. Knox saw in her only feminine guile, and noted disapprovingly her hysterical bouts of weeping. There are, of course, numerous contemporary accounts of her collapsing into prolonged fits of tears at moments of crisis. Living as she did for much of her adult life in circumstances of grave personal danger, that is not surprising, and it is a matter of opinion whether these temperamental outbursts were really just fits of petulance or more seriously the symptoms of panic, fear, despair and frustration: the explanation is perhaps as much medical as historical. Certainly, the image of her as a woman ruled more by the

John Knox. The First Blast of the Trumpet against the monstruous regiment of women. 1558.

heart than the head does not loom large in the literature of the 16th and 17th centuries, preoccupied as it was with dynastic and religious considerations. Apart from conventional references to human frailty, this theme was not strongly developed until the 18th century, when, in their respective histories, David Hume and William Robertson censure Mary for succumbing to indiscreet passions.

Artists, book-illustrators and engravers of the 18th and 19th centuries frequently portrayed Mary in postures that now appear more than a little histrionic, and although the intention may have been perfectly serious, the effect is often the opposite. In this respect, Mary has suffered more at the hands of the artist than has Elizabeth, whose pictorial glorification as the Virgin Queen has been fairly consistent down the centuries. A curious example of the former is an engraving on the titlepage of volume 1 of Robert Keith's *History of the Affairs of Church and State in Scotland*, published in Edinburgh in 1734. The artist has chosen here to portray Mary seated at a table with the infant Prince James at her feet while being admonished by the stern figure of a cleric (presumably Knox). On the floor lie the regalia of Scotland, and above the queen's head a legend reads 'Instability'. Mary's air of resignation does not suggest that she was an attentive listener!

Anti-Marian opinions were capable of arousing strong feelings in the 19th century, as the English novelist Thackeray discovered during a tour through Scotland in 1856. In the course of a historical lecture in Edinburgh on *The Four Georges* he threw in a dismissive comment on Mary which provoked patriotic hissing from a section of the audience led by the Blackwood brothers. Thackeray chose to regard this incident as 'famous sport', since he was lodging at the time with the Blackwoods in Edinburgh. His confidence was boosted by support from Dr John Brown, author of *Rab and his*

Friends, who thanked him for having 'delivered us from Mary Queen of Scots, and Bruce and Haggis, and Burns, and Auld Reekie, and Hugh Miller'.

Accusations of folly rather than wickedness have become common among 20th-century Marian historians, biographers, and dramatists, many of whom adopt a psychological approach. As a theme it occurs in Stefan Zweig's biography *Maria Stuart*, and Robert Bolt's play, *Vivat! Vivat Regina!* It is the interpretation most popular in the cinema and on television where she is usually portrayed as a woman driven by sexual passion and in which the dialogue is often trite and novelettish. Of modern biographers few have been more damning in their indictment of her than D. H. Willson in the opening chapter of his *King James VI and I* (1956). However, even this is mild in comparison with a particularly scurrilous passage from *Scottish Scene, or The Intelligent Man's Guide to Albyn* (1934), by Lewis Grassic Gibbon and Hugh MacDiarmid, in which she is accused of possessing 'the face, mind, manners and morals of a well-intentioned but hysterical poodle'.

'In my end is my beginning'

The enigma of Mary Stuart, which has held the centre of the historical stage for so long, is a cultural phenomenon that is unlikely ever to lose its fascination. As a story, it is simply too good not to be told and re-told. All the classic ingredients for good theatre and fiction are present: beauty, intrigue, violence, religion and sex. At best, it has been elevated into great drama, music, poetry and prose, and at worst vulgarized in cheap romantic fiction. It is a tale at once squalid and terrible, yet noble and deeply moving. Amid the bewildering array of conflicting opinions we should beware of any writer who claims to be wholly impartial and objective. Each generation has judged Mary Stuart according to its own lights. Considering the brevity of her personal reign in Scotland she has commanded a degree of attention which some have thought to be greatly in excess of her real historical importance. This may well be so, but in the realm of the artistic imagination she continues to rank high among the great figures of history, her legend as potent as that of Helen of Troy. This legend is her greatest legacy to posterity. What she did or failed to do has become so much less important than what she represents. Like King Alfred burning the cakes, or Canute bidding the waves to recede, many of the events in her life have passed into myth and folklore, enough to fill volumes of poetry and shelves of novels! Perhaps her best moment is her exit from the stage of history, that unforgettable triumph amid the appalling scenes before the block at Fotheringhay when to all appearances she had lost almost everything – her throne, her country, her son, her reputation and finally her life. Like a fatal magnet she had drawn to their deaths many of the leading figures of her day until she too fell victim to the same seemingly inevitable fate. She still has the power to attract or repel.

From: Robert Keith. The History of the Affairs of Church and State in Scotland. 1734.

The Later Stuarts: James VI & I to Queen Anne

*The noblest prospect which a Scotchman ever sees is the
high road that leads him to England.*

Dr Samuel Johnson

When the son of Mary Stuart anticipated Dr Johnson's advice and took the road to London in 1603 to succeed Elizabeth as James I of England he thereby severed the ancient link between the Scottish people and their monarchy. From that point onwards the Stuarts were to become no more than visitors in the land of their ancestors and were to grow increasingly out of touch with its distinctive political character and separate national culture. With the exception of James I it is doubtful whether any of the later Stuarts were more successful in governing Scotland than their predecessors had been in the days before the union of the crowns. Uniting the two kingdoms did not, in the short term, bring forth the hoped-for benefits of peace and prosperity that many desired. The comparative success of James was later overshadowed and to some extent undone by the mistakes of Charles I and his sons. The constitutional, political and religious upheavals which convulsed the 17th century – the Civil War, the Cromwellian Interregnum, the 'Killing Times' under Charles II and the Revolution of 1688 – all point to an unstable and bitterly divided society, little better than what had gone before.

As in the past, political confusion brought in its wake disastrous cultural repercussions, particularly in the visual arts where the sorry record of destruction in the previous century continued with renewed fervour. This was especially true in Scotland where an absentee monarchy was largely powerless to check the destructiveness of religious fanaticism. Bad as this was, it was perhaps not so serious as the decline in the quality of Scots literature which suffered a major blow with the removal of the court to London and the consequent loss of royal patronage, something which had been so vital an ingredient in the healthy growth of a national literary culture under the early Stuarts. The departure of the court from Edinburgh in 1603 meant that the status of Scots as the language of learning and creative writing would inevitably diminish, although James and his immediate circle continued to converse in Scots. Accompanying this decline was the gradual disappearance of the theatre and of court

*King James entering
London in 1603.*

65

music, both obnoxious to the Kirk which quickly moved in to fill the vacuum left by the departure of the crown. The restraints which the monarchy in England was able to impose upon the iconoclasm of the puritans for much of the 17th century were simply not available in Scotland after 1603. Apart from state visits in 1617 and 1633, and a brief interlude in the 1680s when James, Duke of York and Albany – later James VII and II – held court at Holyrood, there were few opportunities for poets, dramatists and musicians to enjoy patronage and seek advancement north of the border. The drift southwards thus began in earnest, a draining away of talent that has gone on ever since.

While the artists and writers were packing their bags and going in search of the glittering prizes south of the Tweed, many of the Scottish aristocracy who might have been expected to act as patrons were doing the same. The resultant process of anglicization became so powerful that even in the early decades of the century some native poets such as William Drummond of Hawthornden and James Graham, Marquis of Montrose, were already writing in a formal literary style scarcely distinguishable from English courtly poetry. The old vernacular traditions of the poets Dunbar and Sir David Lindsay, and of the Castalians who had gathered around the young James VI, could not develop in this new literary climate, and so Scots as a literary medium atrophied and its usage became mostly confined to the lower classes. As a vehicle of prose it virtually died out, apart from official publications, while Scots poetry went underground, channelling itself into ballads and folklore until its 18th-century revival by Ramsay, Fergusson and Burns. Spoken Scots lingered for much longer even at the highest levels of society, but inevitably its usage led to a kind of cultural schizophrenia, a cleavage between mind and utterance expressing itself in a stilted form of English.

Other factors in Scottish life combined to dilute and weaken the cultural influence of the Stuarts during the century of the dual monarchy from James I to Queen Anne. Chief amongst these was the powerful position of the Kirk, which had developed its distinctive form of Calvinism, a brand of Judeo-Christianity hostile both to the visual arts and to imaginative literature other than that of a purely religious kind. It would be difficult to exaggerate the powerful hold that this mental outlook exercised over the mind of the average lowland Scot throughout this period and for long after. Added to this was the effect of the severance of many long-standing European cultural links and of the dominance of standard English in the printed word, especially in the widely used Authorized Version of the Bible first published in 1611. All of these tendencies worked against the continuance and growth of a distinctive Scots culture which had been developing over the previous two centuries in close conjunction with the Stuart court. A brief glance at Scottish 17th-century printed literature will quickly demonstrate the poverty of creative writing during that era. The evidence shows that Scottish presses were mostly engaged in producing controversial political and religious tracts, many written from a narrow sectarian point of view, often vituperative and generally of little literary merit. This depressing picture is in sharp contrast to what had gone before and indeed to that which was to follow in the next century, the age of the Enlightenment.

The failure of the Stuarts after James I to keep in touch, far less in sympathy, with the changing face of Scottish political and cultural life was to be one of the causes of their eventual downfall. Between the union of the crowns in 1603 and the death of Queen Anne in 1714 the monarchy became progressively divorced from the realities of the Scottish scene, as is the tendency in distant centres of government, and in the end the Stuarts were to pay the full penalty of that divergence and to taste its bitter fruits in permanent exile.

James VI and I: The Scholar King (1567–1625)

Great Britain's Solomon

John Williams, Bishop of Lincoln

That false Scotch urchin

Queen Elizabeth

James VI and I, the ungainly offspring of a tragic alliance, was a survivor. Unlike most of the Stuarts, he kept his throne until a ripe old age, died peacefully in his bed, and bequeathed to his successor two kingdoms living together in a degree of amity that had been unheard of for centuries. From his earliest days he had known violence, conspiracy and treachery. When he was still in her womb, his mother had been exposed to the insults and physical abuse of Rizzio's assassins and had heard the screams of her dying secretary as he was dragged through her apartments. The unborn child survived this experience but, separated from his parents from infancy, taught to hate and despise his mother by his tutor, the embittered George Buchanan, James grew up to be a serious, scholarly, withdrawn and complicated personality, concealing a high intelligence and political shrewdness beneath a veneer of coarseness, timidity and buffoonery. Like Claudius, Emperor of Rome, the contradictions in James's personality have baffled historians and writers down the centuries. In his novel *The Fortunes of Nigel* Scott could not resist poking fun at him, a view shared by Sully who described James as 'the wisest fool in Christendom'. However, despite physical inadequacies, James managed to survive repeated attempts at kidnapping and assassination – the Ruthven raid, the mysterious Gowrie plot, the assaults of Francis Stewart, fifth Earl of Bothwell, and the foreign intrigues of the Scottish Catholic earls. Having out-manoeuvred all his enemies, and sometimes even Queen Elizabeth herself, he was rewarded in middle age with the attainment of his heart's desire, the throne of England, to which he succeeded in 1603. Such a degree of success is

almost unique in the annals of the Stuarts and in stark contrast to the tragic fate of his mother and of the son who succeeded him.

A Learned Prince

James's reputation as King of England has suffered from comparison with the triumphalism of the previous reign, the days of Gloriana. As King of Scots, his timid behaviour after his mother's execution in 1587, which many have considered shameful, does him no credit. However, his intellectual merits, widely recognized during his lifetime, have in recent years enjoyed a revival of interest and appreciation. James is the scholar king par excellence: a prolific writer, theologian, controversialist and poet. Less interested in the visual arts than most of the Stuarts, he is remembered now as much for his learning and his books as for his political achievements, although his writing is often marred by strange eccentricities both of style and of content which have tempted later critics to take them less seriously than they deserve.

His academic education was of the most rigorous kind. Under the stern guidance of George Buchanan, he was taught Latin, Greek, French and Italian, and was given a thorough grounding in Calvinist theology. James's own rueful comment on his schooling is well known: 'They gar me speik Latin ar I could speik Scottis'. The love of learning that he was later to display with such ostentation was inculcated into him both by Buchanan and by the other, and more gentle, royal tutor, Peter Young. A catalogue of the royal

library compiled by the latter between 1573 and 1583 gives an interesting insight into the formative influences that helped to shape the king's mind. By 1578 the library numbered some six hundred volumes, including many books of French poetry which had been abandoned by Mary on her flight from Scotland a decade before. These included Du Bellay, Ronsard, Marot and Salluste du Bartas, some of whose poems James later translated. Curiously, his collection of poetry did not include the major Scots poets Henryson and Dunbar, nor does he seem to have known the work of his ancestor James I. When he began to write verse himself it was to Latin and French models that he looked for inspiration. Predictably, his library contained the usual collection of Greek and Latin authors and important contemporary histories. Treatises on the theory and practice of ruling were numerous, and included Agapetus, Osorio, and of course Buchanan's famous contribution to political theory, *De Jure Regni apud Scotos*. However, what distinguished this collection from most royal libraries of that time was the large proportion of bibles, psalters and works of Protestant theology, such as Calvin's *Institutes of the Christian Religion*. As the most important Calvinist monarch of his day James received many gifts of books from ministers of the Kirk and leading Protestants. Theodore Beza dedicated to James his *Icones* (1580), a collection of short biographies of important Protestant martyrs and reformers, including John Knox and Patrick Hamilton. The frontispiece to this book has an engraved portrait of the young Scottish king, crowned and armed, wielding a sword and clutching an olive branch.

Royal Apollo

When he reached adolescence James began to display his literary talent. Some of his earliest verses show clearly the anti-feminist influence of Buchanan:

> Even so all women are of nature vaine,
> and can not keip no secret unreveild
> and quhair as once thay do conceave disdaine,
> thay are unable to be reconceild.

Possibly this youthful misogynist had been reading Knox! James's prejudices did not lessen with maturity, and for all his life he showed a marked preference for male company. As he grew up and distanced himself from the restrictions of the schoolroom he gathered around him a group of poets and men of letters of whom the leader was Alexander Montgomerie. To him the king accorded the title 'the prince of poets in our land' and eagerly imitated Montgomerie's paradoxical tastes for both sacred and profane themes. Others in this little coterie included William Fowler, uncle of William Drummond of Hawthornden, Sir Patrick Hume of Polwarth, and the musicians Thomas and Robert Hudson. At the centre of this circle James was known as 'King Cupid' and later, when he had earned his poetic laurels, as the 'Royal Apollo'. His devotees were called 'the Castalian Band' or 'the Brethren of the Muses'. Assembling at convivial gatherings the king set his companions literary labours, commanding Thomas Hudson to translate *La Judith* by Salluste du Bartas and, when it was completed, correcting it with his own hand. He also suggested to William Fowler that he translate the *Trionfi* of Petrarch, and although the translation was never printed James wrote a sonnet in its praise. Inspired by Montgomerie he published in 1584 his first book of verse, *Essayes of a Prentise in the Divine Art of Poesie*. This is quite unashamedly the work of an apprentice hand, a slender volume of juvenilia in which the verses are possibly less interesting than the accompanying prose essay upon the technique of writing poetry, *Ane Schort Treatise, conteining some reulis and cautelis to be observit and eschewit in Scottis Poesie*. More than a mere schoolboy essay, this has been described by Dr Helena M. Shire as 'the manifesto of the new poetry of Renaissance Scotland'. A second volume of royal verse appeared in 1591, *His Majesties Poeticall Exercises at Vacant Houres*, composed, as James explained, 'at stolen moments'.

Although James VI is not considered to be a poet of the stature of his ancestor, James I, he did produce a substantial body of work, more than is generally realized. Most of his poems belong to the last two decades of the 16th century before his accession to the English throne, after which he seems to have had little leisure or inclination for writing verse. His style belongs wholly to the Renaissance and is closely modelled on French patterns. It suffers from a tendency

HENRICVS PRINCEPS

Prince Henry.

towards the bombastic, and has been much criticized for its lack of true poetic feeling. His heaviness of touch is particularly evident in the cumbersome *Lepanto*, a poem of about a thousand lines celebrating the naval victory of Christian Europe over the Turks in 1571. However, on occasion he can aspire to something less artificial, as in this epitaph for his faithful servant, John Shaw:

> For as of trewe and noble race thou came
> So honestie and trueth was all thy caire
> Thy kinn was honoured by thy vertues raire
> Thy place of creditt did thy friends defend.
> Then noble mindes aspire and doe not spaire
> With such a life to conquise such an end
> Bot here my inward greefe does make me staye
> I minde with deeds, and not with wordes to paye.

James's importance as a poet is secondary to his crucial role as a patron of poets. Literature in 16th-century Scotland could hardly flourish without patronage, and the nobility of the time were disinclined or unable to provide it. James gave the necessary support, and had he not gone to England in 1603 there might have been no withering away of native Scottish literature.

'God's Lieutenant'

*Kings are . . . Gods . . . his Lieutenants and Vice-gerents
on earth . . . adorned and furnished with some sparkles
of the Divinitie.*

As a writer of vigorous prose James's literary reputation has stood the test of time better than his fame as a versifier. In torrents of verbosity he let loose his natural disputatiousness, resulting in a prodigious output for a busy monarch whose time, one imagines, would have been taken up with more pressing business. Today he is popularly remembered for his treatises on tobacco and witchcraft, but his contemporary fame rested upon his books about kingship. He was the first British monarch to publish his own account of the position and duties of a king, setting out his ideas of divine right in *The True Lawe of Free Monarchies* (1598) in response to threats posed by the rebellious Scottish nobles and the conflicting claims of Kirk and Papacy; most important of all was the need to assert his own right to the throne of England. His language is pithy and direct, a style that he sustained in his next book, the *Basilikon Doron*, published in the following year, a textbook of the practical realities of kingship addressed to his heir, Prince Henry. The tone here is moral and didactic, containing much sensible advice upon the education of a prince, a favourite theme among Renaissance authors. The first edition of 1599 was privately distributed, but upon the eve of his succession to the English throne four years later the first public edition, extensively revised, was issued in Edinburgh and proved a best-seller. It was on sale in London within a few days of Elizabeth's death, and the demand was such that several editions and adaptations were published by English printers in the months following James's entry into London. Foreign ambassadors read it eagerly, sending it to their governments, and it was soon translated into several European languages. Its practical and literary merits were widely admired, and it continued to be popular for many years.

Tobacco

More agreeable to modern taste than James's reaffirmation of the divine right of kings are his attacks upon tobacco. Not so very long ago such views would have been ridiculed, but in the present climate of medical opinion James's opinions seem quite up-to-date. His *Counterblaste to Tobacco* was published in London in 1604, shortly after his succession, and despite the absurdity of some of the prose it was a serious attempt to curb a habit which he saw as a growing social evil. In this tract – for it is no more than a pamphlet – James compares smoking to excessive drinking, and describes graphically its medical and social consequences. Despite much sound sense this royal outburst seems to have made little difference to the social habits of the age, possibly because James's analogy between tobacco

and alcohol was not taken wholly seriously. His fondness for the bottle was well known, and his court was notorious for intemperance, so his audience was not likely to be impressed by hypocritical royal admonitions. His stand did, however, encourage others to take up the cudgels and write in similar vein, though none as picturesquely as in these closing words of the *Counterblaste*, in which he denounces tobacco as:

> a custom loathsome to the eye, hateful to the nose, harmful to the brain, dangerous to the lungs, and in the black, stinking fume thereof, nearest resembling the horrible Stygian smoke of the pit that is bottomless.

Witchcraft

Less appealing to most modern readers but of great interest to his contemporaries was James's fascination with witchcraft. This was not so unsavoury as it might seem now, for an interest in the black arts and a belief in the powers of witches were common among all classes in the 16th and 17th centuries. During the last years of his Scottish reign James gained the reputation of being a witch-hunter, but in fact he had good reason for fearing the activities of devil-worshippers. The climate of post-Reformation Scotland was peculiarly favourable to this kind of mischief, and unscrupulous persons were not slow to play upon popular superstitions in order to embarrass or harm the king. The storm in the North Sea in 1590 that delayed the arrival in Scotland of his bride, Anne of Denmark, was widely believed to have been raised by witchcraft. The trials of the North Berwick witches in 1590–91 terrified the king with detailed revelations of satanic attempts to topple him from his throne, including throwing cats into the sea! More serious were the highly treasonable ongoings of Francis Stewart, fifth Earl of Bothwell who, though of unsound mind, had friends in high places on both sides of the border and in the underworld, sufficiently powerful to enable him to intimidate and terrorize the king with impunity for several years. His sinister involvement with the North Berwick witches and his attacks upon the king, while the latter was in residence at Falkland and at Holyrood, confirmed James's detestation of all those who dabbled in witchcraft. One result of these harrowing experiences was his book, *Daemonologie*, published in 1597. Once thought to be quaint and absurd, it is now treated with a little less scepticism than before. Certainly some of his pronouncements about witches flying through the air cannot be taken seriously, but he is sensible about the need for magistrates to be on their guard against charlatans and to remember their duty to protect the innocent as well as to punish the guilty. The current revival of interest in witchcraft in modern society shows James's book in a new light, and gives it a curious topicality. After he left Scotland for the greater comfort and safety of the English court his interest in witches diminished, and he grew more and more sceptical in his old age, sometimes even preventing convictions in doubtful cases.

Schoolmaster of the Realm

King James, as a sincere lover of learning, was at ease in the company of academics and enjoyed exhibiting his scholarship. He saw himself in the role of the nation's schoolmaster, and wished to be considered the patron of institutions of learning. Although he had little to do with the foundation of Edinburgh University in 1582, he was fond of speaking as if he had been the guiding spirit behind it. Originally known as the 'Tounis College', its title was changed to 'King James's College' by royal command when he paid a visit to Scotland in 1617. To this day the inscription over the main entrance to the Old Quad of the University describes it as James the Sixth's Academy. Having bestowed his name upon the College he also promised it 'a royal God-bairn gift for enlarging the patrimony thereof' and passed an Act in 1621 confirming its privileges and placing the College upon an equal footing with the other Scottish universities. After moving to England he took great interest in all aspects of education, increased the endowments of Trinity College in Dublin, attempted to found a college of divinity in Chelsea, granted substantial benefits to both Oxford and Cambridge, and visited these ancient seats of learning on several occasions. When he visited Oxford's Bodleian Library in 1605 he was generous with offers of gifts from the royal libraries and as a token of their gratitude the University later erected a statue in his honour in Bodley's quadrangle where it stands to this day. Determined to play the dominie he put his influence behind an exceedingly dull little book that appeared in 1615 entitled *God and the King*. This was intended as a textbook for the instruction of children in the obedience owed to their sovereign. In Scotland he commanded that it be taught not only in the schools but in the universities, a reminder perhaps that the Scots were less deferential towards monarchy than his English subjects!

Defender of the Faith

The branch of learning that most interested James, and with which he had a life-long obsession, was theology. No other British monarch can compare with him in this respect, nor equal his output of religious prose and devotional verse. Nurtured from his earliest days as a 'godly prince', reared on biblical theology and Calvinist principles, James was never happier than when engaging in religious controversies and confounding his opponents with quotations from Scripture and abstruse Latin commentaries. His leading Catholic antagonist in these controversies was Cardinal Robert Bellarmine, with whom he grappled in a long and acrimonious literary debate. From his strict Calvinist upbringing sprung a fondness for argument, a rigidity of thinking and an impatience with all other points of view. While he remained in Scotland his absolutist tendencies were kept in check by the stubborn resistance of the Kirk, which was not prepared to bend the knee to any sovereign other than Jesus Christ, and was not afraid to remind James, in the famous words of Andrew Melville, that he was no more than 'God's sillie vassal'. In England James found to his relief a more reverential attitude toward monarchy, and a much more congenial atmosphere in which to dazzle his hearers with his wit and wisdom. His reputation as a scholar king had preceded him. He had already published meditations upon books in the Old Testament to which he later added his commentaries upon the Lord's Prayer and the Gospel of St Matthew. He also translated the Psalms of King David in collaboration with the poet Sir William Alexander, later Earl of Stirling; but his greatest contribution to the religious life of his age, and indeed to the enrichment of future generations, was his encouragement of a new translation of the Bible. The production of the famous Authorized Version was begun in 1604 and completed in 1611, the greatest literary monument of post-Reformation English Protestant scholarship, and one that kept its popularity for over three hundred years. The fulsome praise of the king in the dedication was not undeserved, for he took a close interest in every stage of the translation, made frequent suggestions regarding language and interpretation and approved the choice of translators.

In the Promised Land

The English reigns of King James and the later Stuarts and the rich cultural influence that they exercised upon their adopted country are subjects quite outside the scope of this essay. James VI and I holds a unique position in that he is the only one of his dynasty whose political and intellectual life straddles both countries and both cultural traditions. His English subjects must at first have found him a curious figure, speaking broad Scots interspersed with Latin quotations and outrageous puns, dressed in heavily padded clothes for fear of assassination, possessing uncouth manners and an ungainly figure. However, they were soon to discover his formidable intellectual powers, his sharp wit and his eye for men of letters and learning. He quickly perceived the worth of such men as Francis Bacon, whose literary talents were enlisted for the drafting of the 1604 royal declaration consummating the union of England and Scotland under one crown. The text of this proclamation contains the earliest definition of Great Britain as a national entity, a prophetic document of fundamental constitutional importance. In England James continued on a more lavish scale than before his patronage of men of learning and of leading churchmen, among them Bishop Lancelot Andrewes and the poet John Donne; but the Jacobean court is most remembered for its masques and pageantry in which his queen, Anne of Denmark, took a leading role. This was the court of Ben Jonson, Inigo Jones and, of course, of the twilight years of Shakespeare. The royal children – Prince Henry, who died prematurely in 1612, and his sister Elizabeth, later the 'Winter Queen', who lived to a ripe old age – inherited their father's literary tastes, and were both patrons of literature and objects of poetic adulation. However, their lives and influence scarcely touched Scotland although both were born and brought up there.

The Scottish State Visit, 1617

James was the last of the Stuarts, indeed the last British monarch, to rule Scotland from a position of intimate knowledge. Neither his mother nor his son, Charles I, had this advantage, and both came to grief partly because of it. After James, no Stuart was able to repeat his proud boast that Scotland could be ruled from London with a stroke of his pen (a far from empty claim as the comparative peace of his reign demonstrates). When he left Edinburgh in 1603 on his triumphal progress to London he had promised that he would return every three years, but for various reasons, including English opposition, he did not come back until 1617, the first state visit of a reigning British monarch to Scotland. As a public relations exercise it was a splendid success, though costly, involving extensive repairs at the royal residences in Edinburgh, Falkland and Stirling, and the fitting up of the royal chapel at Holyrood. Tapestries, silver and robes came up by sea from London; roads were improved; and Edinburgh was cleared of beggars to make it more presentable for the royal homecoming. The glamour of monarchy, made all the sweeter by a long absence from its native hearth, stilled the objections of those Calvinists who were offended by the installation of a 'popish' organ in the royal chapel and by James's insistence on Anglican ritual. However, when he proposed erecting gilded wooden statues of the apostles in the chapel the Scottish clergy protested loudly and he yielded reluctantly. Had he ordered figures of dragons and devils, he retorted, the Scots would not have objected! Clearly he knew his countrymen well. Despite this minor setback, the visit went ahead with great rejoicing and much pomp and circumstance. When he crossed the border James was welcomed by grateful verses from the pen of William Drummond of Hawthornden, praying that the king would remain in Scotland:

> Ah why should Isis only see thee shine?
> Is not the Forth as well as Isis thine?
> Though Isis vaunt she hath more wealth in store,
> Let it suffice thy Forth doth love thee more.

The king entered Edinburgh in great style to be greeted with a flowery oration from the city fathers, then within a few days he set off on a triumphant progress through the Scottish lowlands. Everywhere he went he was assailed by elaborate and frequently abominable addresses and poetry, sufficient to fill over 300 pages of a folio volume. One of the more amusing of these literary efforts was performed at Linlithgow, where the local schoolmaster, encased in the plaster figure of a lion, greeted the king in the following words composed by the ever faithful William Drummond:

> Thrice royal Sir, here I do you beseech,
> Who art a lion, to hear a lion's speech,
> A miracle, for since the days of Aesop,
> No lion till these times his voice dared raise up.

> To such a Majesty; then, King of men,
> The King of beasts speaks to thee from his den;
> Who, though he now enclosed be in plaster,
> When he was free, was Lithgow's wise schoolmaster.

Of this episode Robert Chalmers later commented acidly, 'A more farcical incident does not occur throughout the whole life of this farcical monarch'. James, however, revelled in this kind of nonsense, delighting in puns and literary clowning. The Scottish visit had more than its fair share of these royal eccentricities, but they suited contemporary taste, and James returned south well satisfied with the results of his mission. Scotland was not to see him again, and none of his Stuart successors was to enjoy his personal popularity north of the border. Henceforth, the Stuarts were to be as strangers in the land of their ancestors, paying increasingly infrequent and troubled visits, like exiles who feel the occasional urge to return to their roots. Not until the arrival of the Hanoverian George IV in 1822 did Scotland experience another royal visit where pleasure was the order of the day.

Charles I: The Martyr King (1625–1649)

We stand astonished, that, among a civilized people, so much virtue could ever meet with so fatal a catastrophe.

David Hume

Charles Stuart, that man of blood.

Resolution of the Parliamentary Army 1648

Charles I, the last Stuart monarch to be born in Scotland, was the first of his line, since the accession of James IV in 1488, to ascend the throne as an adult. Yet although he took up the duties of kingship in circumstances far more favourable and peaceful than any of his immediate predecessors, his reign deteriorated into a disastrous civil war that engulfed his kingdoms and culminated with his death upon the scaffold in 1649. The fatal star that presided over the destinies of so many of the Stuarts shone fiercely upon the misfortunes of Charles I, and just as the Civil War divided his people into warring camps, so his posthumous reputation and contro-versial political record have divided historians and writers in every generation. Although these controversies have proved less virulent and wide-ranging than those which surround Mary's name, they have nonetheless given him a tragic status, second only to hers, in the history of the Stuarts. The great historic calamities of his reign are largely a matter of English history, but his fate was peculiarly bound up with his native country, for it was in Scotland that he was born, it was Scots who influenced his early formative years, it was to Scotland that he returned in 1633 for his coronation, and again in

1641 in a last vain attempt to retrieve his fortunes, and it was there that the seeds of his ultimate downfall were sown. Whether venerated as a 'martyr king' or abhorred as 'that man of blood' he occupies a special position both in legend and in history, coupled with his undisputed distinction as one of the greatest patrons of the arts ever to sit upon the British throne.

A Godly Prince

Born in 1600 in Dunfermline Palace, the sickly younger son of James VI and Anne of Denmark, the baby prince was not expected to live long. However, against all the odds, he managed to survive infancy and to follow his parents down into England in 1604 after the union of the crowns. Created Duke of Albany and later of York, Charles lived his early years in the shadow of his brilliant, athletic elder brother Henry, until the latter's death in 1612 pushed him into the forefront of public life as heir to the throne. Outgrowing all of his childhood disabilities, except for a stammer and a resultant shyness that many took for aloofness, he matured into a prince whose character and tastes were sharply different from those of his father. Shocked by the coarseness of the Jacobean court, Charles was determined to steer an opposite course. Grave, deeply religious, a faithful husband and devoted father, he ranks high among British monarchs as a paragon of the Christian virtues in his private life. The problem was that his virtues were better suited to church than state.

The 17th century was a deeply religious age, and Charles was in this respect a man of his time, so that any attempt to explain away his failure in purely political or economic terms is inadequate. Like his father, he had a deep interest in theology and a passionate belief in the doctrine of divine right, but there the similarities end. Brought up in easier circumstances than those that James had had to endure, Charles lacked his father's canniness and experience in dealing with the business of government. Though conscientious and diligent, he could also be obstinate and stubborn to a disastrous degree. His political record has won him few accolades from English historians, while in Scotland, with the conspicuous exception of David Hume, even fewer voices have been raised in his defence. Politics apart he is now remembered in England either as an Anglican martyr or as a great patron of the arts, but in the land of his birth his religious influence is widely felt to have been divisive and his artistic patronage is regarded with hostile indifference.

A Royal Connoisseur

Charles was a great art collector. Relying upon agents for purchases abroad he was conspicuous even among his fellow sovereigns for his munificence. He was particularly interested in the Italian masters. Early in his reign he bought Mantegna's great tempera series 'The Triumphs of Caesar', and later, on the advice of Rubens, the Raphael cartoons. Rubens, whom Charles commissioned to paint the ceiling which Inigo Jones had designed for the banqueting hall in the palace of Whitehall, described his royal patron as 'le prince le plus amateur qui soit au monde'. For his services he received a knighthood, as did Van Dyck who was persuaded to settle in England and paint his famous gallery of portraits of the royal family and the court. It is Van Dyck who has stamped for ever upon the popular mind his image of the king as a majestic but sorrowful figure, an image which the Italian sculptor Bernini used as a model for his bust of Charles. So lavish was the king in adorning his palaces with pictures and sculpture that Sir Henry Wotton in his *Panegyrick to King Charles* exclaimed that 'Italy (the greatest mother of elegant arts) or at least (next the Grecians) the principal nursery may seem by your magnificence to be translated into England'.

Coronation at Holyrood, 1633

Charles's magnificent record of royal patronage was not entirely confined to England, but Scotland, being of a more austere religious temper, was hardly fertile soil for his sophisticated tastes. The Calvinist north was not yet ready to receive with equanimity, far less admiration, a Raphael or a Bernini! Charles, however, was anxious that his native country should take part in the cultural and religious renewal that he was attempting to introduce into England. In the visual arts his patronage was mostly felt in Edinburgh, whose status as capital city he was keen to enhance. Partly motivated by a desire to increase the prestige and power of the crown, and to impress would-be dissidents, he set about, early in his reign, making plans for his coronation at Holyrood. Uppermost in his thoughts was the need, as he saw it, to return the church to something of her pre-Reformation splendour both in ritual and in endowment. In preparation for his state visit in 1633 the abbey and palace of Holyrood were renovated and decorated while other public buildings in the capital also benefited from royal attention. The High Kirk of St Giles, divided for various purposes, both secular and ecclesiastical, since the Reformation, was elevated to cathedral status and the partitions that disfigured it removed. As a direct result of these new arrangements the building of the Tron Kirk, designed by John Mylne, one of a long line of architects to the Scottish crown, was begun, and in the immediate vicinity of the cathedral a new Parliament House was erected on royal instructions. This great building was begun in 1632 and completed some eight years later on the eve of the outbreak of the Civil War. Fortunately, its noble interior with its mighty hammer-beamed oak roof still survives, a reminder of the days when a Scottish parliament met in the capital of the kingdom. Less happily, the picturesque façade with its mixture of Scots baronial and Renaissance detail has long since disappeared, hidden behind a rather dull early 19th-century neo-classical exterior, as if anxious to conceal its original political role. Outside Edinburgh, extensive renovations had to be

Parliament House, Edinburgh.

undertaken at the other royal residences of Linlithgow, Stirling, Dunfermline and Falkland, which Charles also visited.

Preparations within the capital were similar to those in 1617 for King James, and ranged from major public works such as the repair of the roads and a thorough cleaning-up of the city down to the practical details of catering for the royal kitchens and necessary sanitary facilities ('chalmer pots and other easments') for guests at the Coronation. James had shown no great personal interest in the visual arts, but Charles was known to be passionately fond of painting and sculpture, so great efforts were made to appeal to his aesthetic tastes. In emulation of the elaborate court masques put on by Inigo Jones and Ben Jonson in London, George Jamesone, the Scottish painter, and the poet, William Drummond, devised a series of tableaux and pageants for the king's entry into Edinburgh. Detailed descriptions have survived of the city streets decorated with triumphal arches, obelisks, paintings and artificial mountains, all displayed to the accompaniment of music. Edinburgh had not witnessed such extravagance since the marriage of James IV and Margaret Tudor. Before the king eventually arrived at Holyrood he had to halt his progress seven times to watch elaborate allegorical tableaux and to admire the handiwork of the city's artists and craftsmen, including a grand arch at the West Port upon which were hung portraits of Scottish kings painted by Jamesone. Half a century later these largely imaginary portraits were used by the Dutch artist Jacob de Witt as models for a similar series to decorate the long

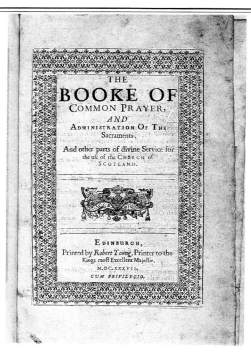

gallery in the reconstructed Holyrood Palace. While Jamesone was busy with his brush, William Drummond, on hand again as in 1617, enthusiastically welcomed his royal master in verse, describing Charles as 'the flower of princes, honour of his time' and declaring that:

> In swelling tides joys everywhere do flow
> By thine approach.

His effusive compliments were matched by the Latin eulogies of Arthur Johnston, whose *Musae Querulae* were wittily translated into English by Sir Francis Kynaston. One of these poems – *Of the rainy weather in England, and the faire in Scotland* – reminds us that the climate was just as important for the success of a royal visit then as now:

> Twice hath bright Cynthia wan'd,
>   twice fill'd her round,
> Since England with continuall raine
>   lies drownd;
> While Spring here winters, Scotland
>   doth behold
> Dayes without cloudes, skies azure,
>   Sunnes of gold.
> Thus whiles the King from Thames
>   to Tweed doth goe,
> One Kingdome smiles, the other
>   weepes for woe.

Another amusing memento of the 1633 visit is the poem *Scotlands Welcome to her Native Sonne* by that compulsive traveller, William Lithgow. Although intended as a celebration, this curious poem is better known now for its complaints about declining moral standards in the northern half of Britain. Among these Lithgow singles out for special condemnation the decay of education, the prevalence of swearing, football, long hair, tobacco, runaway marriages and the immodesty of plaids!

There were, however, other more serious complaints heard in 1633 than those of the rather eccentric Lithgow. For, failing to recognize that Scotland had developed her own distinctive type of Protestantism very different from the more ritualistic Anglicanism of England, Charles insensitively had himself crowned at Holyrood on June 18th in a ceremony, arranged by William Laud, later Archbishop of Canterbury, the splendour of which deeply offended many of his subjects, who were not disposed to distinguish between the king's Anglicanism and Roman Catholicism which they perceived as an ever-present danger.

'Popish' Books

Suspicions of popery were reinforced when the king's printer in Edinburgh, Robert Young, on instructions from Laud, published an edition of the New Testament to coincide with the coronation. The book was richly illustrated with engravings of a decidedly Catholic flavour. These were based upon the work of a Flemish artist, Boetius à Bolswert, who had first issued them in a devotional work on the Passion of Christ published at Antwerp in 1622. His portrayal of the Virgin Mary and the Saints made no concessions to contemporary Scottish feelings and were received with horror. To modern taste this elegant little octavo is valuable not only on account of its historical associations but also as a minor work of art. Illustrated copies of this New Testament are rare, and it can be safely assumed that many must have perished in the wars of the mid-17th century. Repugnant as this religious iconography was to the majority of the king's Scottish subjects, worse was to follow a few years later in 1637 when a new Scottish prayer book was published. Once again Laud played a major part in persuading the king and the Scottish bishops to accept a liturgy based upon the Church of England's Book of Common Prayer. Few books in Scottish history have caused such a furore. The very appearance of this handsome volume, again printed by Robert Young of Edinburgh, with its red and black type, its rich printer's ornaments and decorated capitals was offensive to austere Calvinists. Now valued as a fine example of the typographer's art, its aesthetic merits only served to aggravate popular opposition at the time. However, far more vocal were the objections to what it contained. Despite an attempt to make some concessions to Scottish practices these were nullified by the king's insistence that a proclamation be prefixed to the book, commanding its use by royal prerogative. Other objectionable features were the inclusion of a calendar of saints' days and some chapters from the Apocrypha. The Scottish Prayer Book seems innocuous enough now, but when it was first introduced in St Giles's Cathedral on Sunday July 23rd 1637 it caused a riot, giving rise to the legend of the woman named Jenny Geddes who, the story goes, was so outraged that she flung her stool at the head of the dean for daring to 'say mass in her lug'.

This book proved so unpopular that it was soon withdrawn, but the Scots, now thoroughly alarmed by what they perceived to be the arbitrary and Romanizing tendencies of an absentee monarch whose policy toward Scotland was dangerously influenced by his French Catholic queen and Anglican archbishop, organized themselves into a powerful opposition, and events moved quickly. The National Covenant of 1638 which pledged Scotland to Presbyterianism was the immediate result, provoking the 'Bishops' War' in which the forces of the Covenant won an almost bloodless victory over the king, a victory which in its turn gave heart to his enemies in England, precipitated the Civil War and contributed eventually to his defeat and death.

The 1641 Visit

By the time of the king's second visit to Scotland in 1641 the forces of Calvinism had triumphed over the Carolean attempt to impose an alien culture upon Scotland. Charles, anxious to appease his former opponents in the hope that they would support his cause in England, gave in gracefully to the demands of the Scots for the setting up of a strictly Calvinist church. Absent from this visit was the ceremonial and pomp of 1633; business not pleasure was the order of the day, and such pleasure as there was did not pass uninterrupted. On the day before he left Scotland (November 17th 1641) Charles was enjoying a game of golf on Leith Links when the news of the Irish Rebellion was brought to him. With the troubles of his three kingdoms lying heavy on his shoulders he departed for the south never to return. He was the last reigning Stuart monarch to visit Scotland; his sons Charles II and James VII came north in very different circumstances, but all three revealed in their conduct and policies the seriousness of the gulf that had developed between sovereign and subject: a tragic and destructive clash between two Christian cultures.

Martyrdom and 'Eikon Basilike'

He nothing common did nor mean
Upon that memorable scene,
But with his keener eye
The axe's edge did try.

Andrew Marvell

The Civil War which broke out in England in 1642 was only in part caused by the ecclesiastical situation which had first erupted in

The Marquis of Montrose.

Execution of Charles I.

Scotland and then spread south, but the defeat of the royalist cause brought down with it the Church of England and established Presbyterianism in its place. The failure of the king's military and diplomatic efforts, and his subsequent execution, belong mostly to the pages of English history. Similarly, the literature of martyrdom that grew up after his death in 1649 is part of the history of English literature and found little response north of the border where his death was deplored for different reasons, most Scots regarding it as an affront to their ancient royal house rather than a sacrilegious crime perpetrated upon the defender of the Church. Not many Scots rushed into prose or verse to lament the passing of the 'martyr' king. A conspicuous exception was the royalist champion and warrior-poet James Graham, Marquis of Montrose, whose *Lines on the Death of King Charles I* still convey the passionate grief and desire for revenge felt by many at the time:

> Great, good and just, could I but rate
> My grief and thy too rigid fate,
> I'd weep the world in such a strain
> As it should deluge once again.
> But since thy loud-tongued blood demands supplies
> More from Briareus' hands than Argus' eyes,
> I'll sing thy dirge with trumpet-sounds
> And write thine epitaph with blood and wounds.

However, if Montrose had few imitators among his countrymen, English royalists both at home and abroad were not slow to express their sense of outrage. Within a few days of the execution a book appeared in London with the title in Greek, *Eikon Basilike*. Its sub-

Eikon Basilike (portrait of Charles I by Wenceslaus Hollar).

title explained that it was *The Pourtraicture of His Sacred Majestie in his Solitudes and Sufferings.* Printed by a devoted royalist, Richard Royston, it contained a series of religious meditations, prayers and reflections on the principal events of the king's reign. By royalists it was instantly accepted as the king's own work, and despite Cromwellian attempts at suppression sold in great quantities and reprinted some thirty-five times within the year. As a literary event it was without parallel in English history, but even more significant was its religious and political influence. It created the vision of King Charles the Martyr in which royalists sincerely believed at the time and which many Anglicans still continue to honour. Later in the century controversy about its authorship raised its head, but modern scholarly opinion has come down broadly in support of royal authorship, with the substantial proviso that the responsibility for putting the work together and seeing it through the press, while the king was in prison, was that of a divine, John Gauden, later elevated to a bishopric by a grateful Charles II. Such nice distinctions did not worry monarchists at the time. For them it was a heaven-sent opportunity to deify the king, compare his martyrdom to the Passion of Christ, and denounce his executioners. As a literary manifesto it kept royalist hopes alive in the dark days of the Commonwealth, and to the power of the printed word was added the artist's image of the martyred king in countless engravings and frontispieces prefaced to the text. In these the king is portrayed kneeling in prayer, dressed in royal robes, surrounded by the emblems of martyrdom, and lit by a beam shining from heaven.

Many of these images seem awkward and strained to modern taste, an exception being the engraving by the Czech, Wenceslaus Hollar, where the hand of a skilled artist is more evident than in most.

Scotland played little part in this propaganda war, a conflict in which the chief protagonists all belong to the annals of English literature. The opposition was led by John Milton, at that time secretary to the Council of State. In his *Eikonoklastes* Milton attempted to demolish the image of the king presented in the *Eikon Basilike*, but seems to have had less success than that earlier anti-monarchist, George Buchanan, whose vilification of Mary Queen of Scots had been much more effective. Within Scotland itself there was no great literary or sentimental outcry, no Clarendon to praise nor Milton to denounce, and beyond the circles of devout Episcopalians the king's reputation was never a burning issue in the sense that Mary's was. In general the prevailing view was unsympathetic, as David Hume later discovered when his *History of England* was criticized for presuming 'to shed a generous tear for the fate of Charles I'. Passions, however, could still be aroused, as James Boswell found to his cost when he introduced his hero, Dr Johnson, to his formidable father, Lord Auchinleck, towards the end of their Scottish tour in 1773. As a Tory, Johnson found Auchinleck's Whig principles offensive, and when the contentious subject of King Charles was raised a furious row ensued, despite all the attempts of poor Boswell to steer the conversation into less troubled waters. So embarrassed was he by this incident that his *Life of Johnson* glosses over the details and merely records: 'In the course of their altercation, Whiggism and Presbyterianism, Toryism and Episcopacy, were terribly buffeted'. Boswell also omits to mention his father's brutal retort when challenged by Johnson to say something

Thomas Rowlandson. Picturesque Beauties of Boswell. 1786.

good about Cromwell – 'God, Doctor! he gart kings ken that they had a lith [i.e. joint] in their neck!' This crowning insult was no doubt the moment that the artist, Thomas Rowlandson, had in mind for his satirical drawing of 'The Contest at Auchinleck' in *Picturesque Beauties of Boswell* (1786).

Charles II: The Merry Monarch (1660–1685)

God bless our good and gracious King
Whose promise none relyes on
Who never said a foolish thing
Nor ever did a wise one.

John Wilmot, Earl of Rochester

This is very true: for my words are my own,
and my actions are my ministers'.

Reply by the king to Rochester's epigram

The response of Charles II to Rochester's witty epigram is typical of his outlook, and sums up neatly the character of the merry monarch – amiable, tolerant and cynical. His personality and the whole ethos of his reign are quite different from those of his father, and offer another example of the fascinating diversity of the Stuarts. Easy-going and sensual, he was not a man to sacrifice his comforts for principles, so, unlike many of his line, he managed to make a political comeback, returning from exile to keep hold of his crown in circumstances where a more upright man might have failed. However, if the political acumen which he possessed is not popularly associated with the Stuarts, he did share to the full one family trait: a passionate interest in the arts. In this respect he was truly a Stuart and consequently his reign is important for major cultural and scientific advances.

The Covenanters' King

In 1650, the year following the execution of his father, the young king, realizing that his only hope of restoration lay in Scotland – since both England and Ireland were closed to him and the European powers were slow to come to his aid – landed in the Cromarty Firth and marched south, keeping court at Falkland on the way. Although he was popular with the common people and the army, his worldly, pleasure-seeking nature did not endear him to the stern Calvinists of the Kirk, in whose hands lay the reins of power, both secular and sacred. Yet although he might privately complain that 'Presbytery . . . was not a religion for gentlemen', he was careful to conceal such dangerous sentiments, even swallowing insults to his family by agreeing to sign a humiliating declaration acknowledging his father's guilt and his mother's popish idolatry. The absurdity of his position was caricatured in a contemporary English cartoon in *Old Sayings and Predictions* (1651), showing Charles being pressed, nose downwards, against a grindstone by a black-coated divine from whose lips come the words 'Stoope Charles'.

'Stoope Charles.'

Coronation of Charles II at Scone.

Before his arrival, the Scots had forced him to sign an oath swearing loyalty to the National Covenant of 1638 and the Solemn League and Covenant of 1643. This effectively committed him to supporting the establishment of Presbyterianism throughout Scotland and England, a promise which he never intended to keep, and which in political terms was unattainable, but as an act of expediency it paved the way for his coronation on New Year's Day, 1651. This event took place at Scone in Perthshire, the traditional crowning-place of the kings of Scotland, and was an austere affair, marked not only by an absence of ceremonial, but by a sermon of inordinate length – some two and a half hours – by Robert Douglas, Moderator of the General Assembly. As we know from the published account of the sermon in *The Forme and Order of the Coronation of Charles the Second* (1651), it was severely admonitory in tone – placing great stress on the duties of kingship, the importance of the Covenant, and the sins of the Stuarts – heavily laden with Old Testament allusions. He was the last Stuart to be crowned in Scotland.

The events which followed Charles's hurried coronation at Scone – his march into England, his defeat at Worcester, his amazing escape and flight into exile – are all as much part of the Stuart legend as Mary's flight from Langside or Prince Charlie's escape from Culloden. But throughout the decade of exile before his return to England – his enemies having failed to establish a new political dynasty – Charles was never to forget the humiliations to which he had been subjected in Scotland. Even in the halcyon days after his Restoration, the memory of Scotland could still rouse him to uncharacteristic anger, an emotion which he is said to have assuaged by reading Samuel Butler's *Hudibras*, one of his favourite books. Butler's cynical anti-clericalism appealed to Charles, who was impatient of the disputatiousness that he had encountered in Scotland – 'As if religion were intended/For nothing else but to be mended'!

Restoration

I stood in the Strand and beheld it and blessed God.

John Evelyn

On his triumphant return in May 1660 Charles was received by his English subjects with rapturous joy. As in Europe at the end of the Second World War, supporters and collaborators of the previous regime suddenly suffered a drastic reduction in numbers or wisely went into hiding. The return of the monarchy, after an interval of eleven years, was received with apparently universal delight judging from the flood of adulatory verses, pompous speeches and solemn sermons that flowed from the presses of both kingdoms. In the north the official response was as uncritical as in the south but, one suspects, much less heartfelt and riddled with reservations. Distance may sometimes lend enchantment, but in Scotland after 1660 it merely deepened the gulf between the king and large sections of his people. One Scot, however, did show unqualified delight at the king's return. This was the eccentric Sir Thomas Urquhart of Cromarty, translator of Rabelais, who is alleged to have expired in an uncontrollable fit of laughter upon hearing of the Restoration!

Once he was restored to his throne Charles the ex-Covenanter abandoned his promises to the Presbyterians, assumed his father's title as head of the Church of England and restored episcopacy in Scotland. He further antagonized the Scots by his easy-going attitude towards Catholicism and his loose sexual morals: not what the men of the Covenant hoped for in a 'godly prince'. For his part, Charles looked with distaste upon a country which, viewed from London, seemed to have many of the trappings of a theocratic state governed by religious fanatics. Since he had already been crowned King of Scots he felt no need to re-visit his northern kingdom and in fact never set foot there again.

The forebodings which many Scots felt in the early days of the Restoration were to be fully justified by the events of the next two decades, a period of religious and political persecution and bloodshed which the king did little to alleviate despite his personal inclination toward mercy. It was, on the whole, an unpropitious time for patronage and the cultivation of the arts, at least until the arrival in 1679 of the king's brother James in Edinburgh. The great flowering of the visual arts and sciences that is the most attractive feature of Restoration England was not matched by a similar movement in the north. The absence of the court was, as before, the overriding factor, and it is a matter for regret that Scotland was unable to benefit from closer contact with an enlightened and highly intelligent monarch whose better side showed itself in a love for literature and drama and in a strong taste for architecture and painting. In England this was the age of Dryden, of Restoration comedy, of Sir Christopher Wren, Kneller and Lely. Equally important were the great advances made in the physical sciences, developments in which the king took a major part. In this Charles showed a range of interests not dissimilar to those of his ancestor James IV, dabbling in medicine, attending dissections, performing chemical experiments in a specially-designed laboratory, and taking endless delight in inspecting his navy and receiving reports on shipbuilding. Considering the nature of the king's scientific interests it was appropriate that this was the reign that saw the foundation of the Royal Society.

It would be inaccurate to give the impression that these developments passed Scotland by entirely, but such activity as there was did not emerge until towards the end of the reign. Literature was certainly at a low ebb. The list of titles published in Scotland during those years makes dreary reading and reveals an almost total absence of creative writing. Apart from the reprinting of old classics by such as Sir David Lindsay and Henry the Minstrel, the literary diet of the Scottish reading public seems to have been limited to politics and religion, the latter predominating. As Alexander Campbell observes in his *History of Poetry in Scotland*, 'scarcely anything was relished in Scotland unless it was larded plentifully with the "marrow of divinity"; hence the meagreness of profane productions, in the long lent of innocent hilarity'. In this censorious atmosphere the theatre suffered greatly, perhaps not too grievous a loss considering the repetitive bawdiness of much English Restoration drama. During the 1660s two plays were performed at Holyrood, but not much else escaped the severe scrutiny of the Kirk which throughout this period, and indeed until the late 18th century, regarded the stage as the domain of the devil. This lack of a theatrical tradition had, of course, been a gap in the Scottish cultural scene ever since the departure of the court to London in 1603, and with it had gone the musical and artistic activity that was so strong a feature of the earlier Stuart court.

Printing

The dullness of Scottish Restoration writing was accompanied by a corresponding decline in standards of typography and design in the printing presses of Edinburgh and Glasgow. The robustness and distinctive charm of the Scottish press in the years before the Civil Wars had degenerated rapidly under pressure of demands for mass production during the war of propaganda between the opposing factions. Slipshod press work, slovenly design and poor legibility are the hallmarks of Scottish printing for much of the second half of the 17th century. One might have expected that standards would have improved after the Restoration, but this was not so, and the situation worsened when Andrew Anderson of Edinburgh obtained the gift of King's Printer in 1671 for a period of 41 years. His productions, and those of his widow and heirs, are among the worst ever to proceed from the Scottish press. However, about 1680 the situation began to improve. In the previous year Sir Thomas Murray of Glendoick had secured a royal licence to publish the acts of the Scottish parliaments and made an agreement with an Edinburgh merchant, David Lindsay, to undertake this work. Lindsay entered into partnership with two Dutch printers resident in Edinburgh, Joshua van Solingen and Jan Colmar, and obtained a gift from the king protecting him against the attempts of the Anderson family to enforce their monopoly. The happy result was some of the most impressive work to come out of late 17th-century Scotland, the *Laws and Acts* of 1681 and Sir Robert Sibbald's *Scotia Illustrata* of 1684, both printed in a handsome roman and italic, some of the earliest Dutch types used in Scotland. Neither of these types is found in contemporary English printing, although the italic was later used as a model by William Caslon. Royal patronage was important in introducing the skill of these Dutchmen to Scotland and later, in the brief reign of James VII, was absolutely essential in protecting them against their rivals.

Holyrood

The stirring of the intellectual and artistic life of Edinburgh that took place in the last years of the reign of Charles II owed more to the presence of his brother James in the city than it did to the ageing and increasingly languid monarch in distant London, but to Charles alone must go the credit for the rebuilding in the 1670s of Holyrood, the ancient palace of the Stuarts. A taste for architecture had been strong among his ancestors, and his years of exile in Europe had

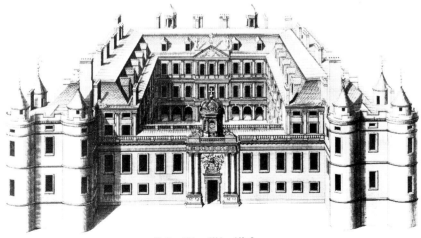

The Royal Palace of Holyrood House

Holyrood.

93

given him an opportunity to become acquainted with the latest architectural styles. In England he is remembered for his splendid additions and reconstruction at Windsor Castle, and for his part in the replanning of London after the Great Fire of 1666. His patronage of Sir Christopher Wren showed also that the king had a keen eye for a man of genius. North of the border the scope for royal patronage was necessarily much more limited, and only in Edinburgh was any major architectural work undertaken. Except for Holyrood, and some repairs at Stirling, none of the other Stuart palaces seem to have benefited much and were for the most part left to moulder quietly into genteel decay. Holyrood, however, was important to Charles not only as a symbol of the monarchy's presence in the capital but also as the principal seat of government and patronage. It had not enjoyed a peaceful history. The magnificent medieval abbey had been reduced after the Reformation to a ghost of its former glory; only the nave continued to be used as a church. The palace of James IV and V had suffered pillaging and burning at the hands of the Earl of Hertford in 1544, but had been partially repaired during the reigns of James VI and Charles I. The latter had proposed a major scheme of rebuilding but this was never carried out, and in 1650, when Cromwellian troops were quartered in the building, the palace was badly damaged by fire. More patching-up ensued, and for a time the inhabitable portions were used as a barracks. After the Restoration a full survey of the palace was made by John Mylne in 1663, and in 1670 the Privy Council voted large sums for a major programme of rebuilding. The architect chosen was Sir William Bruce of Kinross, Scotland's first truly classical architect, who collaborated with the king's Master Mason, Robert Mylne, to produce the restrained classical edifice that we recognize today. The rebuilding took eight years from 1671 to 1679, and throughout its progress the king took a close interest in it, although he was destined never to spend a night within its walls. Bruce received explicit and detailed instructions: 'With all possible diligence you shall demolish and take down the buildings and rooms built by the usurpers above the front of the west quarter and designe and order the building thereof in pillar worke conforme to and with the Dorick and Ionic orders and style'. Bruce retained the old tower of James IV that contains the rooms of Mary Queen of Scots and balanced it with a replica at the south end of the main façade. The inspiration for his designs came from his earlier travels in France where he had read current architectural treatises such as Le Muet's *Manière de bien bastir*.

The dignified austerity of the exterior of the palace belies the opulence of some of the internal plasterwork which was executed by two Englishmen, John Hulbert and George Dunsterfield, with the aid of a Scot, Thomas Alborn. Here the florid heaviness of the Restoration style is seen in its full exuberance. Other parts of the interior decoration were entrusted to two Dutchmen, the painter Jacob de Witt and the carver Jan van Santvoort. The former, although by no means a contemptible artist, has gone down in history as the person responsible for the absurd series of portraits of Scottish monarchs that line the walls of the long gallery that occupies the north wing of the palace. These confections commence with the legendary Fergus I (c.500 A.D.) and terminate with a portrait of James VII and II. The artist was commissioned in 1684 'to make them like unto the Originalls which are to be given to him', and the rate of payment was two pounds each! Looking at them now it is hard to suppress the suspicion that poor De Witt soon ran out of his supply of 'Originalls' and recruited some of the good citizens of the Canongate as models to revive his flagging artistic inspiration. 'A lot of bad portraits', commented Hans Christian Andersen when he visited Holyrood in 1847. Others have been less charitable, though none so violent as the Hanoverian troops who occupied the palace at the time of the Jacobite Rising in 1746 and took out their spite on Prince Charlie's ancestors by slashing the portraits with their swords. Subsequently they were repaired and remounted. When so much that was precious in the Stuart heritage has perished it is supremely ironical that these paintings still survive!

Death

He had been, he said, an unconscionable time dying; but he hoped that they would excuse it.

Macaulay

There cannot have been many Scots who sincerely mourned the passing of King Charles in 1685. An absentee monarch who had not been in Scotland for more than thirty years, his political and religious policies were widely disliked and in the more extreme covenanting circles cordially hated. Even allowing for some exaggeration on the part of later historians, the persecutions of the 'Killing Times' during his reign have left a deep mark on the folk-memory of the Scottish people. Such popularity as the monarchy enjoyed in Scotland was mostly confined to Edinburgh where the presence of the king's brother, the future James VII and II, at various periods during the early 1680s provided a little glamour and a much-needed focus for patronage and the dissemination of courtly culture. Of all the Stuarts Charles II had loved Scotland the least, and had left the government of it to others. It is, therefore, all the more surprising that Edinburgh should have chosen to commemorate him with the erection of a statue in Parliament Close, and even more surprising that it should have survived the vicissitudes of three centuries. This equestrian life-size statue was supplied in 1685 by James Smith, Surveyor of the King's Works, and was an import, probably from Holland. It glorifies the late king who is clad and garlanded like a Roman emperor, proudly mounted on a prancing warhorse on a pedestal situated in the middle of what is now a car park for the law courts, but was formerly the site of St Giles's burial ground. Its erection caused great comment at the time. 'The vulgar people, who have never seen the like before, were much amazed at it', wrote Lord Fountainhall. Modern passers-by are not always aware of the proximity of this statue to the burial-place of John Knox who was interred, if tradition is to be believed, in the ancient graveyard of St Giles within a few feet of the exact spot that was later chosen for this monument to King Charles. Strange that the stern reformer and the merry monarch, whose characters had so little in common, should be such close neighbours right at the very heart of Scotland's capital!

Statue of Charles II in Parliament Square, Edinburgh.

James VII and II (1685–88)

He would have been an excellent King of Spain.

Charles Whibley

James VII has frequently been portrayed either as an ogre or a fool. Whig historians, anxious to glorify the Revolution of 1688 which overthrew the Catholic James and brought in William of Orange, depicted him as a bigot with little political sense; in the 19th century Macaulay sketched him as a vindictive tyrant; while even James's defenders, such as Hilaire Belloc, have not denied that he was to a considerable extent responsible for bringing upon his own head the disasters which drove him from the throne in 1688. For while Charles II knew how far he could go when faced with political realities, and thereby kept his crown, his brother James was oblivious of, or chose to ignore, those realities, and in due course paid the penalty. There is, however, a more positive aspect to James, namely, his cultural influence on Scotland, where its effect was twofold. On the one hand, as Duke of York and Albany, he exercised a direct and mostly beneficial influence on the culture of Scotland, particularly during his residence in Edinburgh from 1679 to 1682; on the other hand, as the partial instrument of his own downfall, he was the unwitting founder not only of the Jacobite movement, but of the vast literary tradition of ballad, song and legend which it engendered. Yet while the importance of Jacobitism as a strand in Scotland's cultural heritage is well known, James's earlier and more direct influence on Scotland has, until recently, received scant attention.

It is only now becoming apparent that the last years of the reign of Charles II were for Edinburgh a period of major cultural and scholarly development, an era when the first stirrings of the Enlightenment of the next century made themselves felt. This cultural awakening owed little, however, to the direct patronage of the reigning monarch, who never ventured outside England while king. Most of the impetus came from the presence in Edinburgh of his younger brother, the Duke of York and future James VII, who came north in 1679 at a time when the nation had for decades been starved of the benefits that in most European countries could only be obtained through the influence of a royal patron. Nobody was more surprised than James by the welcome he received on his arrival in Edinburgh. In the south, his recent conversion to the Church of Rome – at a time when Charles II was trying to contain the hysteria engendered by the fictitious 'Popish Plot' – had made him extremely unpopular, and his second marriage to Mary of Modena, an Italian Catholic princess, had done little to improve his image. The problem was compounded by the fact that Charles had no legitimate heir, thus leaving his brother as his only lawful successor. Furthermore, James had not made things easier by flaunting his faith openly, nor was he helped by a personal manner which lacked the easy charm of his less principled brother. However, none of this prevented his warm reception in Edinburgh, where he was received loyally as a member of Scotland's ancient royal house, and as someone whose arrival might bring pleasing distractions and much-needed colour into everyday life. Besides, the canny citizens of the capital were glad of anything that promised an increase in trade.

James remained in Scotland, apart from interruptions when the king recalled him to London, until May 1682, during which time he visited his ancestral palaces at Linlithgow and Stirling, being particularly impressed by the latter, commenting that 'it exceeded very much all that he had heard of it'. Most of his time, however, was spent at Holyrood, where the newly-built classical palace had just been completed in time to receive him. Ironically, he was to be the last member of the reigning Stuart dynasty to inhabit it, and after his departure no royal court graced its rooms until the coming of Bonnie Prince Charlie in 1745.

During his residence in Scotland, James was the natural leader of the royalist political establishment, which consisted of the gentry, the Episcopalian church (at the time the established religion), and those Catholics who dared to declare themselves openly. He cultivated their loyalties assiduously, and continued to do so after his departure in 1682, at least until the last two years of his reign. The years between 1679 and his final collapse in December 1688 offer a remarkable demonstration of the vital role that enlightened royal patronage can play in inspiring and setting up important new institutions and encouraging existing ones. The Royal College of Physicians, the Advocates' Library and the Order of the Thistle were all instituted at this time, and encouragement was given to the Physic Garden and the Royal Company of Archers. The city of Edinburgh and its University received new charters, and patronage was extended to surgery, cartography, mathematics and engineering. Were it not for the disastrous mistakes of the later years of James's reign and his subsequent failure to regain the throne, these earlier successes would long ago have been given proper recognition.

The Royal College of Physicians

Of all the initiatives launched during that period the establishment of the Royal College of Physicians of Edinburgh was the most successful. It was not an entirely new move, both James VI and Charles I having given instructions for the foundation of such a college, and rules having been drawn up as far back as 1633, but obstruction by pressure groups had delayed progress until the 1670s when the physicians of Edinburgh, led by Robert Sibbald, turned again to the monarchy for support. As Geographer-Royal and Royal Physician Sibbald was high in James's favour, and was therefore in a strong position to persuade him to obtain a charter from Charles II. This was duly granted in 1681. James showed great interest in the new foundation, and in January of the following year attended a debate between the chirurgeons and apothecaries. His friendship with Sibbald and personal patronage of the Physicians marked the beginning of a close relationship between the court and the Edinburgh medical world. Associated with that world was the Physic Garden, percursor of the Royal Botanic Garden, which had originated in the 1670s. Sibbald was closely concerned with the Physic Garden which was an important source of drugs. In its early years it was located near Trinity College Church and was also permitted to use part of the grounds of Holyrood.

The Advocates' Library

Of comparable importance to the College of Physicians was the foundation, about the same time, of the Library of the Faculty of Advocates, an institution which gave birth in this century to the National Library of Scotland. Its establishment was largely the work of one man, Sir George Mackenzie of Rosehaugh, Lord Advocate and prolific litterateur. His literary talents embraced legal and historical writing, philosophical and didactic essays, and romantic prose and verse, earning him the epithet of 'the flower of the wits of Scotland'. And flower he did, at least in the drawing-rooms of Holyrood where he was a great favourite with the court. Outwith those select circles he had a rather unsavoury reputation as a relentless persecutor of the Covenanters, and for this has gone down in history as 'Bloody Mackenzie', a kind of Scottish equivalent of England's Judge Jeffreys. Nevertheless, his importance as the principal founder of the Advocates' Library is indisputable, and his

Sir George Mackenzie.

inaugural speech, the *Oratio Inauguralis*, published in London in 1689, reveals a refreshingly non-partisan spirit and breadth of vision which is hard to reconcile with his ferocious reputation. The exact date of the Library's foundation is difficult to determine, but books were being imported from Holland as early as 1682, and by the time of the publication of Mackenzie's inaugural speech seven years later it was solidly established. Its growth and encouragement benefited from the closeness that existed between James and Mackenzie both during the years when the court was at Holyrood and later when the centre of patronage had moved back to London on the accession of James to the throne.

Pomp and Ceremony

The Jacobite and largely Episcopalian culture that revolved around the court at Holyrood blossomed out not only into formal institutions but also into social organizations and aristocratic ceremonial. One example of this was the ancient sport of archery which had been revived in 1676 with the formation of the Royal Company of Archers, a body which was formally recognized by the Privy Council the following year. From the very beginning it was composed almost entirely of men loyal to the Stuarts, and its new regulations laid great stress on loyalty and patriotism. The Company is in existence to this day, and lends picturesque colour to royal occasions in Edinburgh. Its ideals were possibly influential in persuading James to revive the Order of the Thistle in 1687 as part of a scheme to link a Catholic revival with the pre-Reformation traditions of the Stuart monarchy. This distinctively Scottish order of knighthood ranks second only to the Order of the Garter in the list of British knighthoods, and was considered by some to be of greater antiquity. Whatever the truth of the matter, James took it very seriously, and issued a warrant in May 1687 relating the mythical origins of the order and stipulating that its membership should consist of the sovereign and twelve knights: a clear allusion to Christ and the twelve apostles.

Architecture and Antiquities

The importance of the visual arts had always been a strong feature of the Stuart monarchy in Scotland, but for much of the 17th century the maintenance of standards of artistic excellence in the adornment and repair of the ecclesiastical and secular buildings under the care of the Scottish crown was an uphill fight against the philistinism that had taken deep root in the national psyche. Patriotic pride in the achievements of previous generations was not uniformly shared, and in order to encourage greater interest both Charles II and James VII were keen to have the nation's architectural heritage recorded. By so doing, of course, they hoped to enhance the dignity and power of the monarchy, impress the faithful, and remind their subjects of the glories of the Stuart past. To this end Charles II had entrusted the compilation of the work to a Dutch draughtsman, John Slezer, who had settled in Scotland and become Captain of the Artillery and Surveyor of the Ordnance. Slezer travelled throughout the country from 1678 onwards, preparing etchings of the major royal castles, palaces, towns and other notable buildings. While James was at Holyrood Slezer was given further encouragement in his great task, the first attempt to publish a pictorial record of the historical monuments of Scotland. Progress was slow, and the project was still unfinished when the Revolution of 1688 deposed Slezer's royal patron, but fortunately the new monarchs, William and Mary, were sympathetic, and the first volume was published by royal authority in 1693 with the proud title: *Theatrum Scotiae containing the Prospects of Their Majesties Castles and Palaces*. The book, a work of the greatest architectural and topographical interest, contained 57 views and descriptive text by Sir Robert Sibbald. More volumes were envisaged but never published. Some of the plates are extremely valuable for the detail they provide of buildings which are now completely or partially ruined. Less trustworthy are the extravagant claims made in the address to the reader, singing the praises of Scottish architecture, especially the astounding boast that the medieval cathedral of St Andrews was bigger than St Peter's in Rome!

Town Planning

Other architectural ideas were also circulating at Holyrood, but their realization was postponed by James's departure. The first proposals for the expansion of the ancient boundaries of Edinburgh, the construction of a bridge to the north, and the laying-out of a new town, originated in the ducal court at Holyrood in the 1680s. Towards the end of his reign James granted a charter to the city magistrates empowering them to extend their boundaries and to erect the necessary new streets and bridges. Sir William Bruce, the architect of Holyrood, was instructed to design the first North Bridge, but nothing came of these proposals in the aftermath of the Revolution. Seventy-five years later, when the foundation stone of the first North Bridge was laid by George Drummond, Edinburgh's staunchly Hanoverian Lord Provost, he paid tribute to James, conceding that the city had only begun to fulfil what the Duke of York had originally proposed.

Theatre and Sport

James was neither an intellectual himself nor did he have the expansive personality of his elder brother, so the court at Holyrood might well have seemed a rather formal place had it not been for the softening influences of the royal ladies, principally his wife, Mary of Modena, who compensated for her husband's reserve by giving concerts, balls, supper-parties and by introducing the new habit of tea-drinking into Scotland. Amateur theatricals also flourished at the court where they could be performed well away from the disapproving gaze of the Kirk. To say that it was a lean period for the Scottish theatre would be an under-statement, and such enjoyment as was to be had could only be found in royal and aristocratic circles. In July 1681 the court was joined by the young Princess Anne, the future monarch, daughter of James's first marriage to Anne Hyde. She is known to have taken part in masques, and on her step-mother's birthday in November of that year she acted in a performance of Nathaniel Lee's *Mithridates, King of Pontus*. Her father also had his lighter moments and enjoyed sport, particularly tennis and golf. A story is told of him challenging two English noblemen to a game of golf on Leith Links, taking as his partner a local champion, James Patersone, a cobbler. The duke and his companion won the wager, and with his prize money Patersone bought a large house in the Canongate later known as Golfer's Land. A stone from his house still survives with an anagram of Patersone's name on it.

'No Popery'

This interlude was doomed to be brief. As had so often happened in the past, the Stuarts were fated not to enjoy for long their tranquil pursuit of the muses. The uncomfortable truth was that patronage of the arts was inseparable from politics, and even the most innocuous of royal pastimes could seem controversial. The royalist intelligentsia, both Episcopalian and Catholic, that had emerged in the Edinburgh of the 1680s and which had been linked inexorably to the fortunes of the crown, was to disintegrate in the Revolution of 1688. Some of the responsibility for this catastrophe must lie directly with James himself. The moderation that he had displayed in Scotland soon deserted him once he came to the throne in 1685. After his coronation, his attempts to introduce religious toleration for Catholics and his attack upon the Anglican establishment were to unite his enemies against him on both sides of the border. Difficult though it may now be to appreciate the depth of anti-Catholic feeling in late 17th-century Britain, it was folly for any ruler of that period to ignore it, for the truth was that most British people at that time regarded Catholicism as the religion of dissent, a dangerous destabilizing force that was linked to the threat of foreign domination. In such a heated atmosphere it easily became the scapegoat for all the nation's ills, and passions once aroused could be as ugly as the anti-Semitism of modern times.

'The Second Spring', 1686–88

James, overruling the counsel of moderate Catholics, and ignoring hints from the Vatican that he should proceed more slowly, blindly pressed on with his self-appointed crusade. Nowhere were the consequences of his policy more evident than in Edinburgh where Holyrood, the centre of the cultural renewal of the 1680s, was transformed during the years 1686 to 1688 into a Catholic enclave. For this to happen in Calvinist Scotland was incredible enough. For it to have survived as long as it did was nothing short of miraculous. It was a time which devout Catholics would later remember as the 'Second Spring'. Certainly, the pace of change was swift. In less than three years James established within the palace a printing press, permitted the Jesuits to open a college, and succeeded in evicting the Protestant congregation from the nave of the abbey which was converted for use as the Chapel Royal. These dramatic moves in combination with the emancipation of Catholics from most of the penal laws, granted by the king in February 1687, amounted in the eyes of alarmed Protestants to a programme of 'Papal aggression'.

The brief career of the Holyrood press from 1686 to 1688 is a fascinating bye-way in the early history of Scottish printing. Beginning under the auspices of James Watson senior, who took refuge in Holyrood in February 1686 after a 'No Popery' riot in the city's Grassmarket, it soon passed after his death into the hands of a foreigner, Peter Bruce, who had already made a name for himself by establishing a paper mill at Restalrig. Bruce was appointed royal printer in 1687 and set up shop in the forecourt of the palace. The purpose of all this was quite openly to promote Roman Catholic literature and was supported by orders from the Privy Council to suppress all anti-Catholic books. The imprints of some of Bruce's books describe him as 'Mr P. B. Enginneer and Printer to the King's Most Excellent Majesty, for his Household, Chappel and Colledge'. In less than two years Watson and Bruce produced more than fifty

Prospectus of the Jesuit College at Holyrood, 1688.

The Chapel Royal, Holyrood.

books and pamphlets and possibly others that have perished because of their controversial nature. Not outstanding as examples of the typographer's art, they are nonetheless an interesting departure from the usual run of publications that were being issued by the Scottish press. Some, like Dryden's *Hind and the Panther*, were works of contemporary literature; others, such as Thomas à Kempis's *The Following of Christ* and St Francis de Sales's *Introduction to a Devout Life*, were not the kind of reading likely to be well received in the Calvinist north.

More provocative even than the printing press was the setting up in 1688 of a 'Royal College' under the control of Jesuits and housed within the palace. A prospectus printed by Bruce, *Rules of the Schools of the Royal Colledge at Holy-Rood-House*, assured Protestant parents that all boys would be taught with equal care regardless of religion

and that there would be no proselytism. The curriculum was to
include Latin, Greek, poetry, rhetoric and philosophy. This
pioneering ecumenical experiment was scarcely begun before it was
brought to an abrupt close.

The most ostentatious change of all was the refurbishment of the
splendid medieval nave of the ancient abbey as the Chapel Royal,
principally for the use of the Knights of the Thistle. Choir-stalls and
a throne for the sovereign were designed by Sir William Bruce; a
large organ was envisaged, as were marble pavements and some
imported sculpture – all in a classical style totally at variance with the
glories of the 13th-century nave. On St Andrew's Day 1687 the first
mass was celebrated in the restored Chapel. Mary of Modena
presented silver altar vessels and other rich objects of piety for its
adornment. Outside the carefully guarded walls of the palace the

A South View of the Canongate Kirk with some Neighbouring Buildings

citizens of Edinburgh were aghast to discover that the former Protestant congregation of the abbey had been dispossessed. Fears were expressed for the future of St Giles! However, these changes did produce one excellent result still standing. To accommodate the good citizens ousted from Holyrood the king commissioned the Scots architect, James Smith, to build the kirk that now stands in the Canongate. Although built as a Protestant church the design reflects the mutual religious sympathies of both patron and architect. In the flowing lines of its elegant façade there is more than a hint of continental baroque, and the semi-circular chancel of the interior was not constructed with the reformed liturgy in mind. Shortly after its erection the chancel was blocked up, and remained so until its restoration in the middle of this century.

Revolution, 1688

When the end came to all these dreams it came with terrible rapidity. On December 10th 1688, soon after the news of the king's flight from London reached Edinburgh, a mob attacked Holyrood, vandalized the Chapel, destroyed its new furnishings, and even desecrated the ancient tombs of the Stuart kings. The Jesuit college was ransacked and a bonfire was lit in the courtyard to consume the Catholic literature that had been printed in the palace. Peter Bruce was imprisoned, his press impounded and sold to the Society of Stationers. So ended the 'Second Spring'.

As Winston Churchill commented in his biography of Marlborough, 'Scotland was at once the origin and the end of the Stuarts'. No Stuart ruler experienced this bitter truth more sharply than James VII and II. His reign was the shortest in the history of his dynasty, briefer even than that of Mary Queen of Scots. As with her, a promising beginning had soon turned to tragedy and disaster, but unlike Mary, some of whose mistakes may be attributed to fear and panic, James brought about his own ruin by sheer obstinacy. Scotland, which had given birth to his race and had known him in happier days, rejected him as decisively as did his English subjects, but it was to Scotland that the exiled James first turned for support in his vain attempts at restoration. The story of these and subsequent efforts to regain the throne is the history of the Jacobite movement, a long drawn-out struggle that was to continue far beyond James's own lifetime and well into the middle of the 18th century, a conflict in which Scotland played by far the major part. The Stuarts, who for more than three centuries had acted out their lives at the centre of political power, would henceforth be obliged to accustom themselves to a new role of marginal importance, to decades of frustration and intermittent activity in which dreams would gradually take over from reality. Scotland as the principal theatre of those dreams was in time to prove their grave.

The Canongate Kirk.

The Jacobites : an Epilogue

It was a' for our rightfu' King
We left fair Scotland's strand.

Burns

Jacobitism – the word used to describe the movement to restore King James VII and II to the throne from which he had been ousted by his eldest daughter Mary and her Dutch husband William of Orange in the Revolution of 1688 – was originally used by James's opponents as a term of abuse. Three centuries later it is a term heavily burdened with overtones of romance and nostalgia, so that it is nearly impossible to see its true historical significance through the layers of sentimentality that obscure it. It has given birth to a huge body of literature, almost as varied as that inspired by Mary Queen of Scots, but more often than not it has been treated as a subject better suited to writers of light fiction, than to serious scholars. However, whether as history or fiction, Jacobitism can still arouse deep emotions. For many Scots it represents their country's last serious attempt to assert an independent identity, to reverse the Union of 1707, and in particular to preserve Gaeldom from the destructive assaults of an alien culture. The failure of that attempt and its profound consequences can even to this day stir up feelings of frustrated patriotism or critical scorn.

'The Old Pretender.'

The movement begins with the deposition of James VII and II in 1688 and ends with the death of Cardinal York, last of the Stuarts, in 1807. Between these dates there were five attempts from Scotland to restore the Jacobite claimant to the throne of Great Britain. All failed, but the last, in 1745, came within an ace of success. Nobody can fail to agree that it is an exciting story, and from even a brief glance at the vast body of Jacobite literature it is obvious that few have resisted the temptation to give full rein to their imagination. Quite apart from the ballad-writers and story-tellers with whom it is chiefly associated, it is a theme that has attracted the pens of some of the great names in English, Gaelic, and European literature. In its early stages the literary battle was fought out in the pages of Daniel Defoe, Henry Bolingbroke and Jonathan Swift. Later, writers such as Henry Fielding, Tobias Smollett, John Home and the irrepressible James Boswell joined the fray, while the poets Allan Ramsay, Robert Burns and Lady Nairne immortalized the movement in verses that

Departure of Bonnie Prince Charlie for France, September 19th 1746.

are still loved and sung. In Europe the '45 fired the imagination of countless writers, among them Voltaire. In the 19th century its fading memory became a favourite of novelists led by Scott and a host of imitators, followed by Robert Louis Stevenson and countless others. In the late 20th century passions have cooled and partisanship is less blatant, but the appeal of Jacobitism shows no sign of diminishing.

Killiecrankie and the Boyne

Our thistle flourished fresh and fair
And bonny bloomed our roses;
But Whigs came like a frost in June,
And withered a' our posies.
Awa', Whigs, awa'!

It is important to realize from the outset that the first Jacobites represented only one part of the Stuart dynasty. The Revolution did not in fact get rid of all the Stuarts but simply disposed of the troublesome senior branch of the family whose Catholicism had proved unacceptable to the British people as a whole. The Stuarts were to remain on the throne for another quarter of a century in the persons of King James's two daughters by his first marriage, Mary and Anne, both sincere Protestants and conscientious rulers, but with little love for Scotland. During their reigns a series of calamities within Scotland undermined respect for the London government and fostered the growth of Jacobite sentiment. The immediate result was two abortive attempts to restore King James to his throne. The first, in 1689, is now mostly remembered for the ballad celebrating the Pyrrhic victory at Killiecrankie, in which the Jacobite com-

Mary II, wife of William of Orange.

Queen Anne.

The Scots College, Paris.

mander, John Graham of Claverhouse, Viscount Dundee ('Bonnie Dundee'), met his death:

> An' ye had been what I hae been,
> Ye wadna been sae cantie;
> An' ye had seen what I hae seen
> On the braes o' Killiecrankie.

The second, led by King James himself, ended ingloriously on the legendary banks of the Boyne:

> We'll give our prayers both night and day,
> both now and ever after,
> And let us ne'er forget the day
> King James ran from the water.

The Jacobite Court in France –
Twilight of the Auld Alliance

With the collapse of his hopes James retired to permanent exile in France. Louis XIV generously allowed him the use of the palace of Saint-Germain-en-Laye, near Paris, where his ancestress Mary Queen of Scots had spent much of her youth. The Jacobite Court soon established close relations with the Scots College in that city. This ancient seminary could trace its foundation back to the days of Robert the Bruce in the early 14th century, but since the Reformation it had taken on a new lease of life as a focus for Scottish Catholics and as a centre for scholarship, propaganda and the training of priests. During the course of the 17th century it was incorporated within the University of Paris and moved into spacious new premises in the heart of the city in the Rue des Fossés-Saint-Victor. The chapel of St Andrew was added in 1672. As well as providing accommodation for students these buildings housed a fine library, the major European repository for Scotland's Catholic heritage in books and manuscripts. At the core of the collection were the medieval archives of the archdiocese of Glasgow which had been transported to Paris in 1560 by Archbishop James Beaton in order to save them from the reformers. Added to these treasures was Beaton's own library which had been bequeathed to the College after his death in 1603. With the arrival of the Jacobite exiles these collections were greatly augmented. The Stuart connexion was already strong, for Beaton had given to the College many letters of Mary Queen of Scots, to which had been added from the French royal archives her last letter addressed to Henri III from Fotheringhay on February 8th 1587. This was kept as a relic of the martyred queen, and, after an eventful history, is now in the possession of the National Library of Scotland.

In extending their patronage to the Scots College the Jacobites were continuing a tradition begun a century earlier by Mary herself. During her long captivity in England she had provided generously from her own funds toward the maintenance of Scottish students at the College. Therefore it was but natural that her descendant James VII should in his hour of adversity follow her example. It must have been a consolation for both priests and seminarians to find themselves so high in the king's favour that soon after his arrival in France he chose their principal, Lewis Innes of Drumgask, as his personal advisor. Innes later became almoner to Queen Mary of Modena and to her son. Her armorial stamp is a familiar sight on those books from the Scots College which still survive. Her library, together with other volumes bearing the armorials of her husband and son, was deposited in the College probably after her death in 1718. A more important sign of royal favour was the deposit by James, shortly before his death in 1701, of the official archives of the Jacobite court, some of his personal papers, and his autograph memoirs. The Jacobite archives were particularly precious, containing as they did confidential correspondence of a delicate nature relating to leading families in England. The royal papers, better known as the 'Original Memoirs', were also jealously guarded by the College which was well aware of their highly sensitive political nature. Their existence attracted the attention of literary men to the College in the 18th century, chiefly James Macpherson and David Hume, both of whom were permitted to consult copies but not the 'Original Memoirs'.

The Jacobite court had not been long at Saint-Germain-en-Laye before their interest in the Scots College was greatly increased by the momentous discovery of an important early charter in its archives. This document, a 14th-century charter of Robert II, proved beyond question the legitimacy of the Stuart dynasty and refuted decisively doubts raised a century earlier by George Buchanan and others. It was unearthed by the distinguished historian Thomas Innes, brother of Lewis, a quiet scholar who was on intimate terms with some of the leading French intellectuals of the day, including Jean Mabillon. He also enjoyed good relations with Thomas Ruddiman of the Advocates' Library in Edinburgh. The presence of the two scholarly Innes brothers at the College and the favour of royalty encouraged other Jacobite exiles to donate their papers and books to the College library whose predominantly ecclesiastical character soon began to assume a distinct political flavour. Gifts came from the Erskines of Mar, Francis Atterbury, Bishop of Rochester, the Earls of Drummond and Middleton and many others. The shelves were filled not only with works of devotion but also with the writings of Jacobite polemicists such as Archibald Pitcairne and Chevalier Andrew Michael Ramsay.

The sad fate of this great library during the French Revolution when much was destroyed or dispersed is one of the great tragedies of Scottish letters. Lost forever in the days of Robespierre's 'Reign of Terror' were many of the medieval charters of Glasgow, an untold number of Mary Stuart's letters and the 'Original Memoirs' of James VII and II. The College itself was converted into a prison, the library pilfered, and many of its books sold. Of those that remain most are now in the National Library of Scotland where they were deposited in 1974 by the Scottish Roman Catholic Hierarchy. Previously they had been in the safe-keeping of Blairs College near Aberdeen which in the course of the 19th century had inherited the remnants of the Paris library and what remained of the archives. The original buildings of the Scots College still stand but have never been returned to Scottish ownership. However, the Chapel of St Andrew with its memorial tablets to the exiled Stuarts can still be seen by the interested visitor.

Fireworks display at Scots College, Paris celebrating the birth of the Prince of Wales, June 1688.

James Francis Edward Stuart: The Old Pretender (1688–1766)

God bless the King, God bless our faith's defender,
God bless – no harm in blessing – the Pretender,
But who pretender is, or who the king,
God bless us all! that's quite another thing.

John Byrom

The whole troubled history of Jacobitism might never have happened had it not been for the birth on June 10th 1688 at St James's Palace in London of the Prince of Wales, James Francis Edward, son and heir to the Catholic James VII and II, sovereign of Protestant Britain. Few royal infants have caused such a storm of controversy from the very moment of birth, a birth which gave rise to the ridiculous story, put about by those who wished to discredit the royal couple and their child, that the infant was a changeling who had been smuggled into the royal bed inside a warming pan!

The infant who had been the innocent cause of this constitutional crisis, better known as the 'Glorious Revolution', was scarcely six months old when he was whisked away in the dead of night to the safety of France, never to see England again. He grew up in the exiled court at Saint-Germain-en-Laye to succeed his father in 1701 as 'James VIII and III'. This is but one of the many names by which he is known. Not many princes have been so burdened with nicknames – 'Little Jemmy', the 'Chevalier de St George', the 'Old Pretender', or, more derisively, 'Old Mr Misfortune'.

To James all eyes looked in the early years of the 18th century while the childless Queen Anne sat upon the throne of Great Britain. Anne was supremely unfortunate even by Stuart standards in losing all of her children before she came to the throne in 1702, a personal tragedy that had grave constitutional implications for the Protestant succession. In this situation the activities of James and his court in France became a matter of great importance. However, it was not to England that James looked primarily for assistance but to his ancient kingdom north of the Tweed. Scotland was to be the centre of his operations and it was there that he made three serious bids to regain his crown in 1708, 1715, and again in 1719.

The 1708 'Invasion'

The abortive invasion of Scotland in 1708 is the least impressive and least known of all the Jacobite rebellions. Indeed the '08 is scarcely remembered in the standard history books at all. Part of the reason for this was the prosaic fact that the young James had the bad luck to catch measles just before the invasion was due to begin, so the great adventure had to be postponed until he recovered – just one more example of the legendary misfortune of the Stuarts which Voltaire

LABOUR IN VAIN.

*Anti-Jacobite satire
celebrating the failure
of the 1708 'Invasion'.*

was to comment upon later in the century. Appalling weather and
the unexpected appearance of a superior English fleet dampened
the ardour of the French and sent them scurrying back to Dunkirk.
In the end, the nearest that James came to his ancient kingdom was a
glimpse of the Fife coast at Crail and Pittenweem.

Once the immediate military threat was past, the propaganda war
was stepped up. Gilbert Burnet, Scottish-born Bishop of Salisbury
and a highly successful churchman and politician, gave his literary
skills to the government of the day and found that his services paid
handsome dividends. He had long ago convinced himself that the
birth of the Pretender was a shameful imposture and continued to
maintain this position. More damaging were the innumerable
pamphlets produced by Daniel Defoe whose pen had already been
employed on the side of the Union and whose talents were
invaluable in defending the status quo and asserting the rights of the
Protestant Hanoverian claimant. Although his writings were clearly
anti-Jacobite he chose to give them ostensibly ambiguous titles such
as *And what if the Pretender should come?* or *Reasons against the
Succession of the House of Hanover*. Joining battle on the other side was
that fierce champion of Jacobitism, Archibald Pitcairne, celebrated
physician and Latin poet who had written pious verses praising the
sanctity of James VII's last days. Generally Pitcairne was more at
ease venting his spleen upon the recently re-established Presbyterian Kirk which he satirized in a comedy, *The Assembly, or Scotch
Reformation*. During his lifetime a text of this play was circulated
privately in Jacobite clubs and taverns but it was not published until
1722, by which time the Jacobite threat had receded. A selection of
his Latin verses was published by a fellow-Jacobite, Thomas
Ruddiman of the Advocates' Library, who during a long and
successful career managed to steer his allegiance away from politics

into the calmer waters of scholarship. Both Ruddiman and Pitcairne were members of the 'Easy Club' in Edinburgh, a convivial organization devoted to the repeal of the Union and the restoration of 'James VIII'. They were joined in 1711 by a young poet, Allan Ramsay, whose patriotism found its natural expression in vernacular verse. So pleased were they with this discovery that the club made Ramsay its laureate in 1715, but in the course of that year its existence terminated with the collapse of the next Jacobite rising.

The 1715 Rising

'Tho' Geordie reigns in Jamie's stead,
I'm grieved yet scorn to shaw that;
I'll ne'er look down nor hang my head
On rebel whig for a' that;
For a' that, and a' that,
And thrice as muckle as a' that;
He's far beyond the seas the night,
Yet he'll be here for a' that.

Juggling with words and pamphleteering was all very well, but the exiled James was keen to try his hand once again in Scotland. He had to wait until the death of his half-sister Queen Anne in 1714 before an opportunity presented itself. Here again ill luck dogged his every step. When Anne finally died in August of that year his supporters in England failed to act quickly enough and George, the Elector of Hanover, succeeded to the throne on the basis of his descent from Elizabeth of Bohemia, daughter of James VI and I. With his accession, all hopes of a peaceful Stuart restoration vanished, and plans were made for an armed uprising the following year to depose

Sheriffmuir.

King George. The Jacobite forces had the misfortune to be led by John Erskine, Earl of Mar, dubbed 'Bobbing John' because of his fondness for changing sides. On September 6th 1715, he raised the standard of King James 'VIII' on the Braes of Mar and marched south at a leisurely pace to face the government's army led by the Duke of Argyll. At Sheriffmuir near Stirling the two armies met and fought one of the least decisive battles ever to take place on Scottish soil. Despite an overwhelming advantage of numbers Mar failed to carry the day and Argyll was able to bar his progress south. At various points in this bewildering contest both sides seemed to be on the retreat, a ridiculous situation that did not escape the attention of the song-writer:

> There's some say that we wan,
> Some say that they wan,
> Some say that nane wan at a' man;
> But a'e thing I'm sure,
> That at Sheriff Muir
> A battle there was which I saw man:
> And we ran, and they ran,
> And they ran, and we ran,
> And we ran, and they ran awa' man.

see plates page 8

The outcome of all this dithering was that Mar had to retrace his steps north and wait for the arrival of his royal master who at long last landed at Peterhead just before Christmas with only six companions, disguised as common sailors. After only a few weeks in his ancient kingdom it became clear that the situation was hopeless so James was persuaded to abandon his plans and set sail for France. The '15 was over, and for the next fifty years James was to live out his days in permanent exile, a sad and morose figure, emphatically not the kind that legends are made of. Perhaps this explains why the '15 has never taken hold of the popular imagination, unlike the '45.

The 1719 Rising

There'll never be peace till Jamie comes hame.

With the failure of the '15 the Jacobites in Scotland had no intention of submitting quietly to the new regime in London, but bided their time waiting for a suitable opportunity to strike another blow. In the end all that transpired was a modest force of some three hundred Spanish troops brought over to Scotland by the Earl Marischal and commanded by the Marquess of Tullibardine with the help of some clansmen. The 'invasion', if such it can be called, took place at Kintail on the remote north-west coast of Scotland and was based at Eilean Donan castle at the head of Loch Alsh. When this stronghold was captured by government forces the remnants of the Jacobite army were obliged to face their foes on the slopes of the precipitous pass of Glenshiel. In this most inhospitable of terrains the '19 came to a speedy and comparatively bloodless conclusion. The Spaniards surrendered while the clansmen dispersed to their homes. There were to be no more Jacobite invasions for another quarter of a century.

From this succession of disasters James sought consolation in marriage, and his choice fell upon a Polish princess, Clementina Sobieska, grand-daughter of that famous warrior, King John III of Poland, who had saved Vienna from Islam in 1683. After a perilous betrothal the couple were married in September 1719 and took up residence at the Palazzo Muti in Rome, given to the Stuarts by a grateful papacy. From this union came two sons the first of whom, Prince Charles Edward, was born on the last day of 1720, to be followed in 1725 by Prince Henry Benedict. The future of the Jacobite succession now seemed assured, and all hopes became centred on the person of Charles Edward, the prince who was destined to be the leader of the '45, the final and by far the most serious attempt at a Stuart restoration.

Clementina Sobieska, mother of Bonnie Prince Charlie.

Bonnie Prince Charlie and the '45

He either fears his fate too much,
Or his deserts are small,
That puts it not unto the touch
To win or lose it all.

James Graham, Marquis of Montrose

Prince Charles Edward Stuart (1720–88) is one of those Stuarts, like Mary Queen of Scots, about whom far too much nonsense has been written. As far as Scotland is concerned, his political and military importance is almost totally confined to the years 1745–46 when he blazed briefly across the scene and left in his wake a legacy of bitterness and disillusionment that has not yet entirely vanished. After Mary he is probably the best known of all the Stuarts, but in reality his significance is much less than hers. Despite the extraordinary impact that he made on Scotland and the affection he still commands, despite his legendary charm and good looks, his passion for military fame and personal courage, he was, beneath the dazzling exterior, a flawed hero. For although there ran in his veins the blood of his great Sobieski ancestor, who had repulsed the Turks at the gates of Vienna, events were to show that in Charles the spirit of his forebears flowed not quite strongly enough. As a military commander he was impetuous, and in his private life he seems to have been governed almost entirely by his emotions, with disastrous consequences for all those closest to him, but most of all for himself. This contradiction between the Prince Charlie of the legend and the less glamorous historical facts is rarely reflected in the songs, ballads and poetry forever associated with his name, but can be sensed in the writings of Scott and others whose ambivalence towards Jacobitism is still shared by many Scots today.

It is often said that the '45 should never have happened, that it was doomed from the outset, yet it is this quality of foolhardiness that gives the rising its special fascination. The fact that from such small beginnings the rebellion went on to sweep all before it and get within 127 miles of London has only added fuel to the legend. The tragic dénouement at Culloden and the Prince's dramatic escape across the Scottish highlands and islands to France have given this tale an immortality as imperishable as any of the great adventure stories of world literature. Perhaps it is this streak of the gambler in the Prince that still attracts. For others it is the romantic appeal of a lost cause.

'I am come home'

The sun shines out, wide smiles the sea,
The lily blossoms rarely:
O yonder comes the gallant ship!
Thrice welcome, royal Charlie!

Virtually every step of the '45 is enshrined in legend and celebrated in song. When Charles first set foot upon Scottish soil on the island of Eriskay on July 23rd 1745, it is said that a pink convolvulus fell from his pocket and seeded itself in the ground, in which spot it still grows today. However, he had not come to Scotland to indulge in botanical experiments but was all for pressing on to the mainland, a resolution that was opposed by Alexander Macdonald of Boisdale in whose territory he found himself. When, to his astonishment, Boisdale urged him to return home the Prince gave his famous reply: 'I am come home, sir'. After that, there was no prospect of turning him back and he decided to sail at once for the west coast of Scotland where he landed in the district of Borrodale on the shores of the Sound of Arisaig with his tiny band of companions, the 'Seven Men of Moidart'. At first supporters were slow to come forward, but gradually the Prince's eloquence and charm overcame opposition. It was here that Charles may have met the Gaelic poet Alexander Macdonald who later left an account of the rising in which he describes his attempts to teach the Prince his native tongue. How successful this was is not recorded, but there is a tradition that when Charles raised his standard at Glenfinnan on 19 August the poet recited one of his own Jacobite songs *Tearlach Mac Sheumais* (i.e. 'Charles son of James'). 'Tearlach' was the Gaelic form of the Prince's name used by his faithful highlanders.

The place where Charles set up his standard was in Glenfinnan, at the head of Loch Shiel. Once the small Jacobite army of scarcely more than a thousand men had assembled the flag was raised, and James VIII and III was proclaimed king with Charles as regent. It was an unpromising start, but from this remote and inhospitable terrain the Jacobite army marched on swiftly through Lochaber, picking up recruits as it went, down through Blair Atholl and into

The flight of Sir John Cope.

Perth, which Charles entered on horseback at the head of his troops. The rash adventurer had begun to take on the aura of a triumphant conqueror, and the Bonnie Prince Charlie of legend had been born.

The King shall enjoy his own again

It was but a short step from Perth to Edinburgh via Dunblane, Bannockburn, and Linlithgow. On September 17th, less than two months since his landing in Eriskay, Charles entered the capital, and Holyrood was, for the first time in over sixty years, occupied by a member of the Stuart family. At the Mercat Cross King James was proclaimed with all due ceremonial and white cockades were distributed to loyal supporters. In the evening a state ball was held at the palace. An account of the reception of the Prince by the citizens of Edinburgh is given in the autobiography of Dr Alexander 'Jupiter' Carlyle, who was then a young man. He claims that two-thirds of the men in the city were Whigs and two-thirds of the ladies were Jacobites! Some of the former from whom the Prince might normally have expected support suddenly found pressing commitments elsewhere. Allan Ramsay, Jacobite poet and apparently staunch nationalist, discreetly departed for Penicuik for reasons of health. Thomas Ruddiman of the Advocates' Library, who was all his life a convinced Jacobite, Tory and Episcopalian also retired to the country, to write notes on Lucan! Ruddiman's action is understandable on account of his age. His son, Thomas junior, was less cautious and paid a high price for his involvement in the

THE CHEVALIERS MARKET OR HIGHLAND FAIR

Jacobite newspaper *The Caledonian Mercury* with his imprisonment and early death. In general there was no great rush to join the Jacobite cause and curiosity rather than patriotism was the main motive that fired the excited crowds who surrounded Charles wherever he went. His appearance at this time is recorded by one observer who was later to make a great name for himself in the theatre, John Home, future author of the tragedy *Douglas* and a government man. Home saw the Prince riding in Holyrood Park and described the scene less than enthusiastically in his *History of the Rebellion*.

Prestonpans

The Prince soon confounded both his enemies and the sceptics by winning a series of astonishing victories now immortalized in ballad and song. His defeat of the luckless General Sir John Cope at Prestonpans on September 21st has gone down in legend:

> Hey, Johnnie Cope, are ye wauking yet:
> Or are your drums a-beating yet?
> If you were wauking I would wait,
> To gang to the coals i' the morning.

At a stroke this victory made Charles the master of all Scotland, and obliterated the memory of the long series of reverses that Jacobitism had suffered in the past. After Prestonpans Charles's character is seen at its best, magnanimous in his hour of triumph and merciful toward the defeated – a very different story from the brutal behaviour of Cumberland's troops after Culloden. This is the Prince whom Scott describes so vividly in *Waverley,* dancing at a ball in Holyrood and displaying that legendary charm which inspired innumerable folk-songs such as the one with its familiar chorus:

> An' Charlie he's my darling, my darling, my darling,
> Charlie he's my darling, the young Chevalier.

But he was not everybody's darling. Some observers commented on his air of melancholy, others noted with surprise his shyness with the ladies. Needless to say the Presbyterian ministers had no love for him, and one, the Reverend Mr Neil McVicar of the West Kirk in Edinburgh, went so far as to defy the Prince's request that prayers in divine service should not be said for King George. Standing up in his pulpit he prayed as usual for His Majesty – 'Bless the King, thou knows what King I mean . . . And for this man that is come amongst us to seek an earthly crown: we beseech thee in mercy to take him to thyself and give him a crown of glory'.

Into England

Five weeks Charles spent at Holyrood consolidating his position and gaining new recruits, sullenly overlooked by a beleaguered Hanoverian garrison in the Castle, while in the city, caught between these two opposing forces, the Royal Bank of Scotland carried on business with both sides. This element of unreality persisted throughout much of the '45, and followed Charles as he led his army out of Edinburgh and crossed into England by the western route on November 8th.

All opposition seemed to fade away before the advancing Jacobites. Carlisle surrendered. They marched by Penrith and Lancaster to Preston and entered Manchester without striking a blow, but the sweet taste of success was slowly being soured by the growing realization that the hoped-for response from the English Jacobites was not forthcoming. On December 4th the Prince entered Derby and the rest is history.

King George V is said to have remarked of the Jacobite decision to retreat from Derby: 'Had Charles Edward gone on from Derby I should not have been King of England today'. Opinions vary, but many would agree with him that the Prince's judgement was, on this occasion at least, the right one. Charles must have realized that a rebellion in retreat is doomed and is no rebellion at all. That very element of surprise and audacity that had produced his unbroken run of successes might well have carried him right into the very heart of London, where at the news from Derby there was a run on the banks and the Whigs and George II were in a panic. Cartoons were sold on the streets of the capital forewarning the good citizens of the dire consequences of submitting to popery and of the slavery which would surely follow in the wake of the invader. The English populace was being whipped up into a state of terror with exaggerated tales of the ferocity of the highlanders who were regarded as little better than savages. The anti-Jacobite propaganda with which the novelist Henry Fielding had been entrusted was having its effect, and poor Horace Walpole was beginning to fear that he might have to spend the rest of his days in a wretched attic in Hanover! However, it was not to be. The Prince was overruled by his advisers and his dispirited army retreated across the border to the comparative safety of Scotland where a further victory was won against government forces at Falkirk on January 17th 1746. It was to be the last Jacobite success in a remarkable campaign.

Culloden

Drumossie moor, Drumossie day,
A waeful day it was for me;
For there I lost my father dear,
My father dear and brethren three!

Burns

see plates page 8

No other battlefield in Scotland, not even Bannockburn, can evoke such mixed emotions as the windswept field of Culloden, or Drummossie Moor as it was sometimes called. It is impossible for any Scot even after the passage of over two centuries to view it without regret on the one hand or satisfaction on the other. The battle fought in this place on April 16th 1746 dealt the death-blow to the Jacobite cause. Much of the blame must lie with Charles, who, buoyed up on a wave of false optimism generated by his long run of successes in the field, showed a serious lack of judgement in choosing to face the Hanoverian army in unfavourable conditions and against the advice of his most experienced officers. The result was total defeat and carnage, and although the Prince displayed personal bravery he was obliged to withdraw and flee with a small band of devoted followers. What is not always remembered is that this was the only battle that Charles ever lost and the only victory that his foe, Cumberland, ever won.

The Memorial Portrait of Mary as Martyr Queen.

Top-right inscription:

ARIA SCOTIÆ REGINA GALLÆ DOTARIA REGNOR
ACLIÆ ET HYBERNIÆ VERE PRINCEPS LEGITIMA
IACOBI MAGNÆ BRITANIÆ REGIS MATER, A SVIS
OPPRESSA AN DNI 1568 AVXILII SPE ET OPINIONE A
COGNATA ELIZABETHA IN ANGLIA REGNANTE PMISSI
EO DESCENDIT, IBIQVE CONTRA IVS GENTIVM ET
PROMISSI FIDEM CAPTIVA RETENTA, POST CAPTI
VITATIS AN. 19. RELIGIONIS ERGO, EIVSDEM ELIZ
PERFIDIA ET SENATVS ANGLICI CRVDELITATE,
HORRENDA CAPITIS LATA SENTENTIA NECI
TRADITVR, AC 12 CAL. MARTII 1587 IN
AVDITO EXEMPLO A SERVILI ET ABIEC
TO CARNIFICE TETRVM IN MOREM CA
PITE TRVNCATA EST. ANNO ÆTATIS
REGNIQVE 45

Left, beneath crucifix scene: ANLA FORINGHAMIÆ

Left inscription block:

REGINAM SERENISS. REGVM FILIAM,
VXOREM ET MATREM, ASTANTIBVS
COMMISSARIIS ET MINISTRIS R.
ELIZABETHÆ CARIFEX SECVRI
PERCVTIT ATQ VNO ET ALTERO
ICTV TRVCVLENTER SAVCIATÆ
TERTIO EI CAPVT ABSCINDIT,

Right labels: IOANNA KENNETHÆ — ELIZABETHA CVRLE

Bottom banner:

PRIMA QVOAD VIXIT COL. SCOT. PARENS. ET FVND.

Bottom inscription:

SIC FVNESTVM ASCENDIT TABVLATVM REGINA QVONDAM
GALLIARV ET SCOTIÆ FLORENTISS INVICTO SED PIO
ANIMO TYRANNIDEM EXPROBRANT ET PERFIDIAM.
FIDEM CATOLICAM PROFITETVR, ROMANÆ ECCLESIA
SE SEMPER FVISSE ET ESSE FILIAM PALAM PLANE TESTATVR

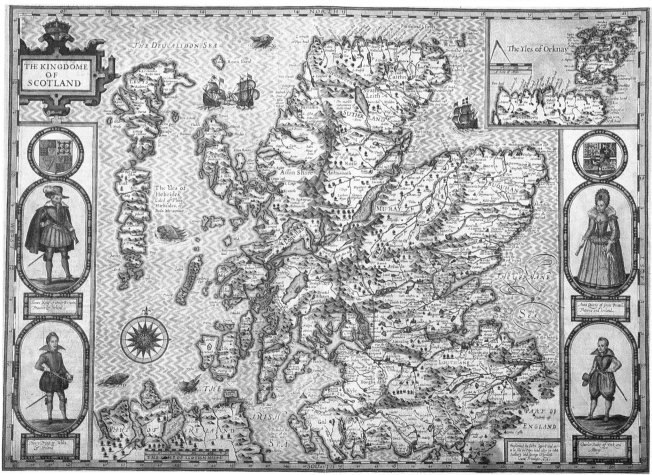

GILDER ROY in his GENUINE HIGHLAND GARB

XIV Miles to EDINR.

LONDON, Sold by S. W. Fores, No. 3, Piccadilly.

The *BATTLE* of **CULLODEN**, near Invernefs in *SCOTLAND*, 16.th April 1746.

*The Kings Army Commanded by the Duke of Cumberland was drawn up in three Lines, into the left of which the Rebels attempting to break with
Swords and Targets were repulsed; when Kingston's Horse attack'd the left Wing, and the Dragoons the Rear, which compleated the Rout of the
Rebels, who had 2500 Men kill'd in the Battle, 1500 in the Pursuit and 1800 taken Prisoners.*

Duke of Cumberland.

*The Old Pretender
landing at Peterhead*

The battle had been fairly won by Cumberland and the men under his command, but what followed is one of the least creditable pages in British history – a campaign of terrorization and confiscation, the destruction of the clan system, and a brutal and sustained assault upon Gaelic culture. Bishop Robert Forbes in his *Lyon in Mourning* relates many legends about deeds of heroism and of savagery committed in the immediate aftermath of the battle, but of one thing there can be no doubt, and that is the personal responsibility of the Duke of Cumberland for the indiscriminate slaughter that ensued. No quarter was given to the wounded or dying, many of whom were bayoneted where they lay or rounded up and incinerated alive. Atrocities continued long after the action was over, and neither age nor sex was spared. An English historian, Lord Mahon, claims that the cruelty shown by Cumberland's troops was 'such as never perhaps before or since has disgraced a British army'. This brutality was a measure of the fear felt by the government at the near success of the rising, and gives the lie to those who would seek to belittle the significance of the '45. However, even on the Hanoverian side voices were raised against Cumberland. A story, possibly aprocryphal, is told of the young Major James Wolfe, later to make a name for himself on the Heights of Abraham and at this time serving under Cumberland. Ordered by the Duke to shoot a wounded Jacobite lying on the battlefield he replied, 'My commission is at the disposal of your Royal Highness, but I cannot consent to become an executioner'. True or false, the story is in keeping with the character of the man who has gone down in history as the 'butcher'.

When Cumberland returned to London he was given an ecstatic welcome. Handel's music hailed the advent of 'the Conquering

Culloden.

125

Hero', bonfires were lit and fireworks set off. Special medals were struck, and Tyburn, grim scene of executions for treason, was appropriately enough re-named Cumberland Gate. Less fittingly the flower 'Sweet William' was called after him, in answer to which some Scots ascribed the title 'Stinking Willie' to a particularly noxious weed.

The Prince in the Heather

It is with a sense of relief that one turns from the slaughter after Culloden to the behaviour of the fugitive Prince and especially of his loyal followers as they fled across Scotland in the months that followed. Hostile propaganda has for long decreed that the highlanders of this period were uncouth barbarians and that the object of their devotion was little better than an effete nincompoop who later showed his true colours by sinking into debauchery and philandering. This does not accord with what is known either of the restrained conduct of the Jacobite army during the '45 or of the Prince's cheerfulness and fortitude during the five months when he was on the run. This was his finest hour, better even than in the days after Prestonpans or before Derby, and it is this which still keeps his memory alive despite his own attempts to bury it in the miserable long years of exile that lay ahead. Like Charles II after Worcester, he was at his best in moments of supreme danger, skulking in the heather, living rough in the most primitive conditions, disguised on one occasion in female dress, often within earshot of his pursuers and escaping detection and death by a hair's-breadth. Brave as he was, his companions and protectors were even braver, and none more so than Flora Macdonald of South Uist who came to his aid when his fortunes were at their lowest ebb. This young woman is no mere legendary heroine. Her quiet courage is well attested, both at this time and later in her eventful life, and she can rank beside any of the heroines of the resistance movements of modern times. Her services to the Prince are all the more impressive because of the total absence of any romantic attachment between them, and so she fully deserves Dr Johnson's generous tribute as 'a name that will be mentioned in history, and if courage and fidelity be virtues, mentioned with honour'.

This period of the Prince's life is the part most beloved of Jacobite and in particular Gaelic poets, but admiration was not totally confined to his supporters, as contemporary literature clearly shows. In the months and years after Culloden the presses of Britain and Europe poured out a stream of pamphlets, histories and verse narrating the adventures of the hunted Prince. In some he is admiringly disguised as 'Young Juba', in others as 'Ascanius or the Young Adventurer', as 'Manlius', 'Alexis' and 'The Wanderer'. The list is endless. Europe rang with the story, so that when Charles finally escaped from Scotland at the end of September 1746 and arrived shortly after in France he was acclaimed as a hero and given a glittering reception by Louis XV and the entire French court at

see plates page 7

Versailles. Far better for his reputation had his life ended at this point, for the next forty years were to be wasted in bitter exile, futile plotting, unseemly quarrels, and a slow decline into drunken oblivion. For much of that time his exact movements were not known and rumours abounded of his supposed return to England on several occasions, one of which is fictionalized in the pages of Scott's *Redgauntlet*. The true story is sorry enough, so that by the time of his death in 1788 all but the most deluded were convinced that the 'Good Old Cause' was truly dead. Whatever was best about that cause Charles seems to have left behind him in the glens and mountains of the Scottish highlands where his memory is still cherished and the songs that he inspired still sung.

Prince Charlie in disguise.

The Cardinal King: Henry Benedict Stuart, Cardinal Duke of York (1725–1807)

*Henry IX, King of Great Britain; not by the will of men
but by the grace of God.*

If in laying claim to this royal title on the death of his elder brother in 1788 Prince Henry showed a surprising ignorance of Scottish history it is understandable considering that he never set foot in the country throughout his long life. He lived entirely abroad where his chosen career and pious character raised him to great heights in the Roman Catholic Church. His controversial decision to enter the Church was taken shortly after the disaster at Culloden had convinced him that the Jacobite cause was dead, a conviction not shared by his more worldly but unstable brother. Created cardinal by Benedict XIV in 1747, Henry advanced rapidly in the Roman Curia and held a number of important posts during the reigns of five popes. Although he never failed to champion his family's cause at the Vatican he is chiefly remembered as a benefactor of the poor, a reforming prelate and a constant patron of the arts. Within Rome he was a conscientious benefactor and protector of the Scots College in that city, while nearby at his see of Frascati he was active in introducing reforms at the local seminary which was restored and enlarged at his expense and further equipped with a printing press and a stage for classical and modern drama. The cardinal's greatest pride was his library, which was housed in the seminary and soon attracted scholars from far and wide. Much of this great library still exists and is now kept in the Vatican to which it was removed during the Second World War in order to save it from the Allied bombardment of Frascati.

The cardinal's literary interests seem to have been highly unusual for an 18th-century Italian prelate. In addition to the customary lives of the saints and works of devotion his tastes ranged widely over architecture, geography, gardening and music (the last particularly dear to his heart). However, a peculiar feature of his library is the great number of books on English and Scottish history and literature, including Gaelic. Some of these he had no doubt inherited from his parents and possibly also from the Stuart court at Saint-Germain-en-Laye, particularly a splendid vellum manuscript illustrating the arms of the kings of England from antiquity until the time of his father as Prince of Wales. Many of the cardinal's books are magnificently bound in red morocco and stamped with the Royal Stuart arms surmounted by a cardinalatial hat.

Apart from being a collector and recipient of fine books the cardinal also indulged in some literary composition himself, notably his little-known treatise, *The Sins of the Drunkard*, in which he warns against the evils of the bottle, written no doubt with his elder

The Stuart monument in St Peter's in Rome, designed by Canova and erected in 1819 to commemorate the last resting-place of the Old Pretender, Bonnie Prince Charlie and Cardinal York.

brother in mind! He was not, of course, the first Stuart to denounce intemperance, for his ancestor James VI and I had long ago in his famous essay on tobacco compared smoking to excessive drinking.

Cardinal York's claim to the title of King of Great Britain after the death of Charles was purely a symbolic gesture, and he was never a serious threat to George III. The real threat lay elsewhere in the impending violence of the French Revolution, which not only involved Britain in a long and bloody war but also threatened to destroy the Roman Catholic Church and drive the aged 'Henry IX' and last of the Stuarts from his domains. In the ensuing chaos he was reduced to poverty from which the British government generously relieved him by granting a pension to which the grateful cardinal later responded by bequeathing to the British crown some of the jewels of his grandfather, James VII and II. These jewels were eventually deposited in Edinburgh Castle beside the Scottish Regalia where they remain to this day. The extensive collection of Stuart family papers belonging to the cardinal at the time of his death in 1807 also found their way, after many an adventure, to Britain where they are now divided between the British Library and Windsor Castle. With the death of this kindly and peace-loving prince of the Church the long and far from peaceful history of the Stuarts finally came to a quiet and most uncharacteristic end.

ACKNOWLEDGEMENTS TO ILLUSTRATIONS

The illustrations on plates pages 2 and 3 are reproduced by gracious permission of Her Majesty the Queen. Other illustrations are reproduced by kind permission of: plates page 1, Bibliothèque Nationale, Paris; plates pages 5 and 6, the Trustees of Blairs College, Aberdeen; page 88, The British Library; page 111, the editor, The Innes Review; pages 57 and 68, National Galleries of Scotland; Frontispiece, Opera della Metropolitana di Siena; plates page 5, Österreichische Nationalbibliothek, Vienna, page 53 Scottish Catholic Archives, Edinburgh.

HMSO publications are available from:

HMSO Bookshops
71 Lothian Road, Edinburgh EH3 9AZ   (031) 228 4181
49 High Holborn, London WC1V 6HB   (01) 211 5656 (Counter service only)
258 Broad Street, Birmingham B1 2HE   (021) 643 3740
Southey House, 33 Wine Street, Bristol BS1 2BQ   (0272) 24306/24307
9-21 Princess Street, Manchester M60 8AS   (061) 834 7201
80 Chichester Street, Belfast BT1 4JY   (0232) 234488

HMSO Publications Centre
(Mail and telephone orders only)
PO Box 276, London SW8 5DT
Telephone orders (01) 622 3316
General enquiries (01) 211 5656

HMSO's Accredited Agents
(see Yellow Pages)

And through good booksellers

Printed in Scotland for HMSO by McCorquodale (Scotland) Ltd.
Dd 287055/HF4680   C50   5/87